BARBARA HEPWORTH

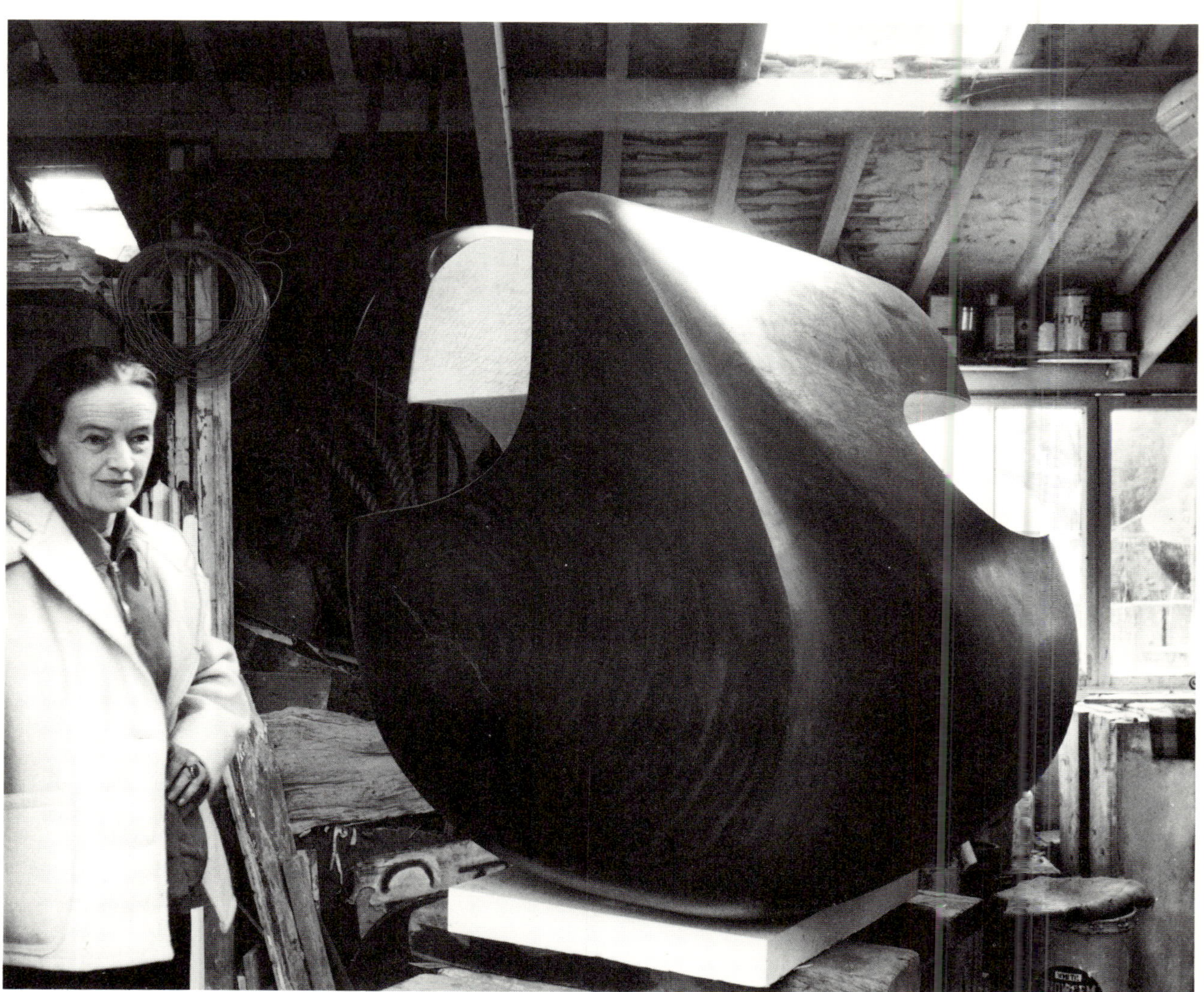

Barbara Hepworth

A guide to the Tate Gallery Collection at London and St Ives, Cornwall

The Tate Gallery

ISBN 0 905005 83 X
Published by order of the Trustees 1982

Published by the Tate Gallery Publications Department,
Millbank, London SW1P 4RG
Designed by Caroline Johnston
Printed by Balding + Mansell Limited, Wisbech, Cambs

Contents

frontispiece
Barbara Hepworth with
Corinthos (1954–5), St Ives

cover
The Sculpture Garden
St Ives, Cornwall

Preface

The Tate Gallery's collection of sculpture and drawings by Barbara Hepworth is displayed in two venues – at the Gallery in Millbank, and in the artist's former home at St Ives in Cornwall.

This is appropriate, because it allows the work to be seen in two contexts. At the Tate, Hepworth takes her place as one of the most innovative artists of the twentieth century, among the first to create a body of consistently abstract sculpture. She is clearly seen as a fine craftsman, always responsive to the qualities of her materials and with a sense of form, classical in its purity and its eschewal of all inessentials.

In St Ives, the sculpture is shown in Trewyn Studio and Garden, where the artist lived and worked during the latter part of her life. Many pieces now on display were made there, and were placed in the garden (which she created) by the artist herself. The workshops remain substantially unchanged, and visitors can appreciate the environment in which Hepworth made her sculpture. This environment extends of course beyond the studio to the West Penwith landscape, and in particular to the wild moorland and coastal scenery, the sea and wave movement that was the inspiration of so many of her sculptures. The figure in the landscape, man's century-long harmonious relationship to nature – this is the Romantic side of Hepworth's work that came to the fore in Cornwall and complements the classical austerity of her earlier sculpture.

Barbara Hepworth had a close and happy relationship with the Tate Gallery. She served as a Trustee from 1965 until 1972, and was most generous with gifts of her work from 1964 onwards. A memorable retrospective exhibition was held at the Tate in 1968, and she was able to supervise the display. When she died in 1975 she expressed the wish to her Executors that her studio and garden should be preserved as a small museum, and that this should eventually pass into the care of the Tate Gallery. This was finally achieved in 1980, giving the Tate its first outstation beyond Millbank.

This guide illustrates all the sculptures, paintings and drawings by Barbara Hepworth in the Tate collection, both in London and St Ives.

Alan Bowness *Director*

Introduction

For the monograph 'Carvings & Drawings' which Barbara Hepworth herself prepared for Lund Humphries in 1952, she divided her output of work into six periods of time, each of about three years, and characterised for each her particular aims. In this *Guide* her whole career is divided into four periods, each of about a decade, which more or less correspond to different preoccupations in her work and life. The first of these comes to a forced and untimely break and a decisive one, with Hepworth's move to Cornwall at the outbreak of war in 1939. It starts with the carvings that were included in her first exhibition, at the Beaux-Arts Gallery in 1928, and includes her discovery of a purely geometrical sculpture and her gradual increase of its variety and scale.

During the war for some years Hepworth was not able to make any sculpture, and for the decade from 1945 she did not produce at quite the same rate as she had during the 1930s. A series of woodcarvings she made then – represented here by 'Pelagos' – are amongst her best, and although abstract they refer directly to the Cornish landscape, appearing in her work for the first time. The following decade, centred on 1960, marks her most productive period and is well represented at the Tate Gallery and St Ives. She had begun to work in metal, in addition to wood and stone, in 1955–6, at first with constructions and then with cast bronze. This enabled her to make a greater number of sculptures and also to invent different kinds of shapes, particularly those suggesting movement. The retrospective exhibition at the Whitechapel Gallery in 1954 (the first of two) and her visit to the Greek islands in the summer of that year mark the beginning of this period. This visit inspired the series of the largest wood carvings, begun in 1955 and made from African hardwood, here represented by 'Corinthos' and 'Epidauros'. Her reputation, and consequently the demands for her work, was now considerable. She received a number of public commissions and in 1964–6 several exhibition tours abroad organised by the British Council.

In the years from 1968 to 1975 Hepworth returned to some of the ideas for sculptures she had had during the 1930s, and again used geometrically simple shapes. The surfaces are usually highly polished, unlike her work before the war, and she used a very dark slate and coloured marbles, giving the sculptures a variety of surface colour that was quite new.

Each piece of sculpture by Barbara Hepworth, throughout her career, has to be understood in part as its subject, whether figure or landscape, and in part as a shape or arrangement of shapes. There is always a balance between these two, at times more abstract and at times more naturalistic. The abstract was always the more difficult to appreciate and at first was quite unexpected. She believed that it was necessary to develop a particular sense in order to respond to solid shapes, or 'forms', and that this response once cultivated was immediate and profound, and the basis for the strength of her work. This idea came slowly during the late 1920s, and was worked out amongst a small circle of artists in London, all of them also frequent visitors to Paris. From 1928 to the mid-1930s there was an increasing emphasis on shape at the expense of detail in her carvings, and alongside this she and others developed two associated ideas, that of the determining role of the physical material of the sculpture, and that of the mission of the artist, as innovator and spiritual leader.

I

The first mature work of Barbara Hepworth, made in the late 1920s, continues some of the concerns of the most advanced sculptors in Britain before 1914, Jacob Epstein, Henri Gaudier-Brzeska and Eric Gill. The interruption of the First World War had caused a gap, prolonged beyond 1918, so that this tradition was not taken up by artists for some ten years. The attraction was not the short-lived pre-war Vorticist style, but the emphasis on direct carving in stone, as opposed to modelling clay to be later cast in bronze. Associated with this was a revulsion against the realistic sculpture made in Europe since the Renaissance, and, consequently, a respect for the primitive and pre-Renaissance. The leader in this interest was Henry Moore, who was five years older than Hepworth. He was also from Yorkshire, and they had met for the first time as fellow students at Leeds School of Art. In 1921 they both entered the sculpture school at the Royal College of Art. When Hepworth left in 1924 she was awarded a travelling scholarship that she chose to spend in Italy, in Florence, Siena and Rome, staying until late in 1926. The two years in Italy were of the greatest importance in her training: the monumental poses of Masaccio's figures can be seen echoed in her own life drawings and many of her sculptures. In Rome she took practical lessons in carving marble, which had not been taught in London, and worked alongside John Skeaping, also a former sculpture pupil at the Royal College, and who was then an assistant to a professional carver. Hepworth and Skeaping were married in Florence in 1925.

At their first public exhibition, at the Beaux-Arts Gallery in the summer of 1928, Barbara Hepworth and John Skeaping exhibited a similar range of sculpture, almost all stone and wood carvings, together with drawings. To exhibit so many carvings, in contrast to modelled clay or plaster, amounted to a manifesto, in which they joined Henry Moore who had similarly exhibited carvings and drawings earlier in the year. 'Torso' (1928), included in the 1928 exhibition, and 'Infant' (1929) are already characteristic. The attraction of the natural surface of the material in each case, acting as a smooth skin, is revealed by the polishing and the gentle curves, and each makes slight turns away from the symmetrical. The simplification in the shapes is a natural result of direct carving and is seen in the work of other sculptors interested in this revival – Eric Gill and Frank Dobson as well as Henry Moore – but the reticence and underplaying of expression are unique.

The third of these early carvings, 'Figure of a woman' (1929–30) of pink stone, is also similar to contemporary work by Henry Moore, who in 1929 had moved to Hampstead, very near the Skeapings who were at 7 The Mall, off Parkhill Road. However similar the pose, the large limbs and the mask-like face, the mood of the figure is utterly different, self-contained within uninterrupted rhythms, and in contrast to the expressive distortions of Moore.

These early carvings of Moore, Hepworth and Skeaping became known slightly later than the similar interest in carving of several artists, including J.D. Fergusson, Richard Garbe, Alan Durst and Charles Wheeler. None of these were so extraordinarily dedicated to the medium, and after the event it can be seen that they did not look for the identification of subject and shape that were also associated with direct carving.

The early 1930s were for Barbara Hepworth the vital years during which she was able to lift the level of her work out of the shadow of Epstein and Gaudier-Brzeska to the abstract style that is typical of all her later work. She worked alongside Henry Moore and Ben Nicholson, and it was with Nicholson particularly, who became her second husband, that she shared her interest in the organic simplicity of the shapes of her carvings. As a painter of still lifes and landscapes his example encouraged her to leave the almost exclusive concern of earlier British sculptors with the human figure.

These three artists in London became the leaders of an avant-garde, both in the sense that their work, as it became more rigorously abstract, was in an extreme style and that they were at the centre of a succession of groups, although Moore at times exhibited with others. They visited and learnt from an earlier generation in Paris, particularly Picasso, Braque, Arp, Brancusi and Mondrian, at a unique time when these artists in their fifties were accessible and still inspiring. The international avant-garde was re-forming in Paris, and they contributed to it as equals. Hepworth's introduction to artists in Paris came partly from Nicholson; in much the same way in later years she travelled rarely and then only if necessary, perhaps to attend an exhibition, in spite of the fact that the experience of travel was so important to her.

The small 'Seated Figure' of 1932–3 is a striking change from the 'Figure of a Woman' of 1930, a change that parallels Henry Moore's work in these years. The flowing design is used by Hepworth to suggest the shape of the original tree trunk, and the way in which the trunk contains the figure, which is correspondingly withdrawn. The profile, incised into the heads of several sculptures from 1932, resembles the drawn profiles in paintings by Ben Nicholson. The mood of 'Seated Figure', a personal and introspective development of some features common to the work of Moore and Nicholson, is seen also in her first geometrically abstract works, made from late in 1934. Nicholson's white reliefs of incised circles date from the same year, as does Henry Moore's 'Four piece composition: reclining figure' in the Tate Gallery. These sculptures and reliefs, including several assemblages of 'Three Forms' by Barbara Hepworth, reacted not only with each other but also with geometrically simple works by Picasso, Brancusi, Arp and Giacometti. Between 1933 and 1935 Hepworth was a member of the group of abstract artists in Paris 'Abstraction-Création', and exhibited there with them. If Moore's sculpture is a figure, and Nicholson's reliefs are completely non-objective, then Hepworth's *Forms* are, at least to begin with, in between. She wrote herself that it was after the birth of her triplets in October 1934 that there was a change in her work:

> 'When I started carving again in November 1934, my work seemed to have changed direction although the only fresh influence had been the arrival of the children. The work was more formal and all traces of naturalism had disappeared, and for some years I was absorbed in the relationships in space, in size and texture and weight, as well as in the tensions between the forms. This formality initiated the exploration with which I have been preoccupied continuously since then, and in which I hope to discover some absolute essence in sculptural terms giving the quality of human relationships'. (Herbert Read, 1952, section 3)

In fact the change was only of degree, and there is an evident continuity with her earlier carvings. Despite the geometry it is still the 'quality of human relationships' that gives life to the sculpture. There is an association between the carvings and her own children, but one with a very private reference which she wrote of in the same text as 'the family group and its closely knit relationship'. The wider association expected from the geometrical shapes is contained in the use of the word 'Form', which she included in the titles of her sculptures from this year.

The word 'form' in art criticism in Britain was associated with the simplified shapes used by the post-impressionist painters, particularly Cézanne, and is appropriate to Barbara Hepworth's early work such as 'Figure of a Woman'. In her first published text, an interview in 'The Studio' in December 1932, she goes further and writes of 'form' as a quality that sculpture may have independently of subject but linked to its particular material, 'the abstract conception of form imbued with that life force'. The critic Herbert Read wrote similarly of her work at the same time, that its beauty came from the combination of expressive shapes with expressive material, 'stone and wood yield their essences to give form a concrete significance' (in catalogue A. Tooth & Sons, November 1932). This link between shape and material was regarded by the sculptor as the key to her work at the time, and is implicit in the use of the word 'form'. In 1934 she again wrote of the need for public 'understanding of form and colour in the abstract' and the corresponding need for the artist to make the relation between abstract forms convey an emotion.

The mid and later 1930s were a productive time for Barbara Hepworth, in which she was able to build on the abstract style of 1934. That the work was almost all on a small scale followed from lack of patrons, particularly necessary in sculpture, and opportunity. Some of the carvings she regarded as projects for larger pieces. Many of them are conjunctions of related abstract shapes, but some, like the tall 'Single Form (Eikon)' (1937–8), are the single shapes themselves. The most severely geometrical of all she made in 1935, such as 'Discs in Echelon'; subsequently the shapes became again more complicated, either organic or sharply crystalline. One of the most angular of these carvings, and closely related to the series of 'Three Forms', is the teak 'Ball, Plane and Hole' (1936). Her exhibition at the Lefevre Gallery in 1937 included both this and her largest pre-war sculpture, the stone 'Monumental Stele' (1936), in which she also used sharp rectangular shapes. The principle of an assembly of shapes on a flat plane remains, but they are varied and in this case each one, and the spaces they leave, are in fact wedges (apart from the circles) and there is a sense of activity and movement between them. Eventually these more mechanical and artificial shapes did not become more than an occasional interest in her later work, although she did sometimes return to them.

The international character of her work and Nicholson's was expressed in the publication 'Circle' in 1937, which was subtitled 'An international survey of Constructive Art'. This illustrated work of British abstract painters amongst the European, but the dominating section was on architecture. The cooperation between painter and sculptor, exemplified by Hepworth and Nicholson, had been enlarged to include architect and designer. The sculptor Naum Gabo had moved to Hampstead, near Hepworth and Nicholson, in 1936, and his interests inspired this extraordinarily ambitious – and in the long run successful – attempt to put through the implications of non-objective art into the widest scale. Henry Moore was not involved, since his work was recognised as essentially figurative, with his qualities of dramatic human expression, and although Barbara Hepworth's wood and stone carvings were crisply geometrical it appears now that fundamentally her work also is not constructivist. Vital to her work of the 1930s are the feeling of handcarving and the deviations from exact geometry that can only be organic: the swelling profile of 'Discs in Echelon' or the lack of symmetry of 'Forms in Echelon', for example. Unlike Gabo she was not interested in synthetic or transparent materials for sculpture.

Another not quite geometrical work, 'Forms in Echelon' (1938) of tulip wood, became later a model for many of the one part and two part sculptures. The connection with both versions of 'Three Forms', particularly in the way they stand on a rectangular base, as well as with 'Discs in Echelon', is clear, but the geometry of the shapes is far more complex, and the ridges and shoulders seem to be pressed from beneath the surface as if over a structure of bones. This is her only pre-war work in the Tate Gallery collection with a hole from side to side, but this was common then in her work and had first featured in it in 1931. Here the hole differentiates one form, slightly taller and dominating, from the other, which has in comparison a narrower foot and a single plane face.

The optimism expressed in 'Circle' was, in the short term, disappointed by the war and, preceding that, by a decline in patronage that was already barely adequate. The final developments in Barbara Hepworth's work of this phase were two further pictorial enrichments, the use of bright colours, painted over concave surfaces, and stretched strings, representing drawn lines. The painting of the sculpture was a startling innovation, and she remained alone in this until a younger generation of sculptors painted their metal constructions. The use of stretched strings corresponds to the ruled lines on some of her drawings of the late 1930s and also, as in their use at the same time by Henry Moore, follows the example of the Russian constructivist Naum Gabo. 'Sculpture with Colour, Deep Blue and Red' (1940) is the smallest of a number of versions of this subject, made as plaster maquettes, and which were the only sculptures she made during the earliest years of the war, after she and her family had left London and moved to Cornwall.

II

The war had a decisive effect on Barbara Hepworth's career. In the first place it occasioned her move from London to St Ives, where she continued to live for the rest of her life. This move seems in retrospect to have been ideal, to the right place and out of London at the right time for her own independence, but the immediate effects following from this must have been disruptive: she made very little sculpture during the war and for the following ten years produced comparatively slowly, although she did then make some of her finest work.

The decision to move from London was made hurriedly and as a necessity to take the family away from the danger of bombing. St Ives was already known to Ben Nicholson, who worked there first in 1928, when he and Christopher Wood had taken an interest in the self-taught painter Alfred Wallis (whose work Barbara Hepworth later also collected). It was chosen now since they were able to stay at Carbis Bay in the large house of Adrian Stokes, the painter and critic who had long been a close friend. They were there for four months from August 1939 until they moved into a small house of their own, eventually moving again into a larger house with rooms suitable for studios in September 1942. Hepworth, in her early forties at the end of the war, was no longer a part of an avant-garde, and she did not again belong to any art group, except for that of St Ives. Her style was far from static, however, and the immediate change that came into it was the incorporation of landscape into her sculpture.

To live in the country was to some extent for her a return to her childhood in Wakefield and Yorkshire. The landscape of St Ives is remarkable for the primitive feel of the cliffs and hills of the Penwith peninsula towards Land's End, with many tumuli and ancient settlements, and always, of course, for the views of the sea. The clarity of the light was important, reminding her of her visit to Provence in 1932, as was also the opportunity to carve out of doors. The suggestions of landscape in her sculpture corresponded with a weakening of the element of pure abstraction. The process began with the artist's noticing a similarity between her already existing works and the Cornish landscape and in this her attitude was comparable to Mondrian's in Manhattan in 1940, recognising a similarity between the grids of his painting and the street pattern of New York.

One of the finest of these landscape sculptures is 'Pelagos' – meaning 'The Sea' – of 1946, and two sculptures in the collection in versions of different materials to the originals can be seen as preparatory to it. 'Oval Sculpture (No.2)' (1943) elaborates the theme of 'Sculpture with Colour, Deep Blue and Red' (1940) in a way which has to do with the clear light of the landscape, particularly in the original wood carving, where the white painted interior is contrasted to the bare, polished wood. 'Landscape Sculpture' (1944), a later bronze cast from the elm carving, and the first to imply a landscape in the title, is still more strongly horizontal, and therefore like landscape, in format. Although these sculptures are similar to her abstract drawings and to the pre-war work, there begins to be a feeling of surface incident between one part and another, as if they were to be viewed topographically, stressed in 'Landscape Sculpture' by the strings, gathered into intersecting cones like rays of sight falling into an eye. Barbara Hepworth wrote in 1952 of experiencing an interior feeling about the landscape at this time:

> 'The colour in the concavities plunged me into the depth of water, caves or shadows deeper than the carved concavities themselves. The strings were the tension I felt between myself and the sea, the wind or the hills.'
> (Herbert Read, 1952, section 4)

This difficult concept, that the artist experiences the landscape in its relation to her, lies behind the idea of an abstract landscape sculpture. This interior feeling for both the landscape and the sculpture were mediated for her by two other factors. The first was her experience of dancing, in which the formal pose of body elevates everyday movements – this was always a factor in her regard for her work, since it related to the way in which she herself felt inspired to behave in the dramatic Cornish landscape; the second the criticism of their neighbour Adrian Stokes, whose interest in psychoanalysis led him to emphasise the association between the body and landscape, and an integral relationship between the body and our response to art.

'Pelagos' (1946) incorporates landscape quite directly into the shape of the sculpture:

> 'A new era seemed to begin for me when we moved into a larger house high on the cliff overlooking the grand sweep of the whole of St. Ives Bay from the Island to Godrevy lighthouse. There was a sudden release from what had seemed to be an almost unbearable diminution of space and now I had a studio workroom looking straight towards the horizon of the sea and enfolded (but with always the escape for the eye straight out to the Atlantic) by the arms of land to the left and the right of me. I have used this idea in *Pelagos* 1946.'
> (Herbert Read, 1952, section 4)

The features of St Ives Bay are quite literally found within the egg-like shape of the complete wooden sculpture that the surface compels one to imagine, and which would resemble one of her abstract sculptures of ten year earlier.

Despite this group of wood carvings, Barbara Hepworth's exhibitions of recent work at the Lefevre Gallery in London in 1946 and 1948 both included more drawings and paintings than sculpture. There were both practical (lack of material for sculpture) and economic reasons for this. In 1947 she made designs for sculptures of reclining figures for the pedestals on Waterloo Bridge in a competition organised by the L.C.C. In the event there was no commission (the pedestals are still empty), but the drawings submitted are on loan to the St Ives Gallery. In the late 1940s there came a change in her subject matter, and for a time she left landscape for sculptures of highly abstracted figures. This was preceded by developments in her drawing, and she began numerous life studies of the female nude, and furthermore a series, which must have seemed a startling departure, of drawings of hospital staff at work in an operating theatre. The hospital subjects were dependent on a fortuitous opportunity in that she was able to witness a number of operations. Her fascination for them came from her observations of the controlled way in which these groups of people moved while actually performing the operations. The control was comparable to that of dancers; the array of tools for cutting into the surface of the body was comparable to her own activity in sculpture. The Tate's 'Fenestration of the Ear (The Hammer)' (1948) was made from sketches made in hospital, and the surgeon's use of mallet and gouge makes this the most relevant to sculpture of the hospital drawings. Hepworth attended many operations and made more than fifty drawings of this theme between 1947 and 1949.

The translation into sculpture of this interest in relations between figures appeared first in a carving from a single stone of two figures, the tall 'Bicentric Form' (1949). This has a close connection with life studies of two standing girls, seen so as to overlap each other within a single outline, similar to the drawing 'Two figures with folded arms' (1947) in style. The sculpture should be viewed as two figures standing one behind the other. The circumstances were here no more than a studio drawing, but the opportunity to extend the idea of the hospital theatre drawings followed from Barbara Hepworth's observation of people in St Mark's Square in Venice, which she visited in the summer of 1950. She was fascinated by the effect that the formal architecture of the square seemed to have on people moving within it:

> 'They walked differently, discovering their innate dignity. They grouped themselves in unconscious recognition of their importance in relation to each other as human beings.' (Herbert Read, 1952, section 6)

She was eventually to think of her sculpture as inspiring in the onlooker the same reaction as did the architecture of the Venetian square, and to be a mediator between the human and architectural scales. At first, however, she made three sculptures of groups of figures, with people in Venice as the point of departure. In each of these one of the stones is on its side, and in the Tate's 'Group I (Concourse), February 4 1951' this is clearly a reclining figure amongst the adults and children. This sculpture is similar to the series of 'Three Forms' of 1934–5, but where there had been a connection with her family the reference is now to an anonymous group. Barbara Hepworth headed the section in the monograph of 1952 which was about her work from 1949 to 1952 'Artist in Society'. She implies that the forms in 'Concourse' are also the community of St Ives, and an image of her own moral commitment and gift to that particular society. In works like 'Pelagos' she had incorporated the landscape into abstract sculpture, but she now felt that the landscape context, evident in the light and material of the sculpture, enabled her to present figures as a coherent group. Her interest in groups of abstract sculpture became increasingly expressive from the simplicity of the 'Three Forms' (1934–5), to the 'Groups' of 1951 inspired by Venice to one of her latest works, 'The Family of Man' (1971), a group of nine bronzes, in which the separate figures are individually characterised and titled.

From shortly after the war Barbara Hepworth had also made coloured drawings of groups of abstract figures, using right angles and rectangles to link the figures together, and including just sufficient features to make glances and gestures understandable. 'Two Figures (Heroes)' (1954) at St Ives is the largest of these, and was occasioned by the death of her son Paul Skeaping on active service with the RAF in Thailand; the two figures refer to him and his co-pilot. He is also remembered by a 'Madonna and Child' in the Lady Chapel of the Parish Church of St Ives, a carving made in 1954 and given in his memory to the church. Specific subjects, although they are frequent in Hepworth's work, are only rarely known, and memorials in abstract art are also rare. This painting is heroic in scale and positive in its presentation of the two figures, but differs otherwise from similar drawings only in the unexplained detail that one of the figures is holding a Hepworth pencil drawing.

III

In the ten years from the mid 1950s to the mid 1960s Barbara Hepworth's reputation, increasing since her exhibition at Venice in 1950 (which was also the date of the Tate's first acquisition of her work), became a factor in all that she did. The demand for her work led to public commissions that gave her at last the opportunity to work on the scale and in the architectural and popular context that she had always sought; this also meant that she had to work with other people, both patrons and dealers and her own assistants. In 1952 Lund Humphries published a study of her work, edited by Herbert Read but with revealing texts by the artist. In 1954 and again in 1962 retrospective exhibitions at the Whitechapel Gallery showed her range, and in the later one the major departure of her later career, the use of bent metal and bronze, was dominant. In 1959 she won the first prize at the Sao Paulo biennale. Following her move in 1949 to the house and rambling studios with the only large garden in the middle of St Ives, Trewyn Studio, she habitually made work of a larger size than before, and in 1961 she also acquired the very large (if incongrous) space of the former 'Palais de Danse' across the road, to use as a workshop and storeroom.

The decade began for her with a series which now counts, with the post-war landscape sculptures, as her outstanding work, a number of large carvings in Nigerian hardwood with subjects inspired in part by the Greek landscape. These also illustrate that her position was by now conservative: while abstract artists of her own generation (Victor Pasmore, Kenneth Martin) and the younger generation from Reg Butler to William Turnbull were in different ways using metal and assemblage, she almost alone continued to rely, at first totally, on the personal touch of the carver's hand. She visited Greece and the islands in August 1954, immediately after the first Whitechapel exhibition. She later wrote of sketching at the classical sites, and of her study of the association between classical sculpture (and architecture) and the landscape. Shortly after her return to St Ives she acquired – apparently partly by mistake – a consignment of very large pieces (up to two tons each) of African wood. She wrote of her work on these 'I was never happier'. 'Corinthos' (1954–5) was the first completed. The size of the blocks enabled her to use a shape neither predominantly figure nor landscape, although the sculpture retains the cylindrical shape of the trunk, placed on its side. The extraordinary quality of this and the other carvings is the sense of light and rhythm in the interior shape tunnelled through the wood. The sheer size of the block gives the physical sensation of exploring the shape with hands and body. In 'Corinthos' Barbara Hepworth plays particularly on bi-lateral symmetry and the single, spiralling line in three dimensions, as with Pelagos, and there is a tension between the evident weight of the block and the apparent airiness of the drawing in space that links the apertures.

The dramatic interior of 'Corinthos', and the comparable drawings of the mid 1950s, are the links between the carvings and Barbara Hepworth's first metal sculptures. She had used bent metal rods earlier in designs for the theatre, Electra (Old Vic, 1951) and for the first performance of Tippett's *The Midsummer Marriage* (Covent Garden, 1955), in both cases to give the impression of free-

dimensional drawing. In the following year she used cut metal sheets in two ways. At first in 'Orpheus' (represented in the collection by 'Orpheus (Maquette 2, version 2,)' 1956) and 'Stringed Figure (Curlew)' (1956), a brass sheet was cut and bent, tensioned by strings, into a continuous surface that resembles both the interiors of some of her carvings and also the drawings of networks of ruled chords within a continuous perimeter. Secondly, 'Forms in Movement (Pavan)' (1956) (cast 1967) extends the principle of the cut surface and continuous outline to a shape neither carved nor bent. Here the metal is used as an armature, and fattened with plaster. With this new material Barbara Hepworth uses for the first time the word 'movement' in the title. The earliest of her cast bronzes in the collection is 'Curved Form (Trevalgan)' (1956), in which the metal again retains a reference to beaten sheet metal and also to the interiors of the wood carvings. She wrote of this sculpture in 1956:

> 'This "Curved Form" was conceived standing on the hill called Trevalgan between St.Ives and Zennor where the land of Cornwall ends and the cliffs divide as they touch the sea facing west.
>
> At this point, facing the setting sun across the Atlantic, where sky and sea blend with hills and rocks, the forms seem to enfold the watcher and lift him towards the sky.'
> (in catalogue, Holland Park Sculpture Exhibition, 1957)

A photograph of her, with her head on her hands inside the sculpture (and which was later used for the cover of a booklet on her by Michael Shepherd) illustrates the meaning of her note, and this is one of several instances in which her own posing beside her sculptures, with the grace of a dancer, reveals directly her attitude.

Bronze casting not only made it possible to make more sculptures but released her from stone-like and tree-like shapes. Her immediate use of shapes implying movement in 'Garden Sculpture (Model for Meridian)' (1958) and 'Cantate Domino' (1958) was followed by further landscape sculptures, or, more precisely, coastscape sculptures. The horizontal shapes of 'Sea Form (Porthmeor)' (1958) and 'Bronze Form (Patmos)' (1962–3) retain references to waves, shells and erosion and the vertical 'Torso II (Torcello)' (1958) was envisaged by the artist in front of the sea, like the Venetian island of the title, and as it often appeared in published photographs of it at Trewyn. To some extent from the later 1950s the differences between the materials of her sculptures became less important, as did the strict adherence to a certain scale for each particular idea. With the help of her assistants she began to make plaster copies of some of the carved sculptures and to cast them in bronze, particularly of wooden sculptures that had begun to crack. For larger bronze sculptures she made maquettes, and also cast these, as with 'Square Forms' (1962), which is a twelve inch study for the eight foot high 'Square Forms with Circles' of the following year. This bronze was remarkable in introducing another range of forms into her work, since she had not previously used squares or rectangles, so much a feature of De Stijl and Nicholson paintings in her sculpture – except for bases and the early and anomalous 'Monumental Stela' (1936). The variety of scale within each subject followed partly from her straining throughout the sixties and early seventies to find the appropriate scale and setting for public sculpture. Whereas earlier it had finally been the surface of her sculpture that was all-important, in later years the setting, and the more distant view typical of the public gaze rather than that of the connoisseur, mattered most.

Wood carvings became exceptional, as most of the sculptures were stone or bronze. 'Figure (Nanjizal)' (1958) is named after a cove near St Ives, and derives from the association between herself as subject and the beach with its cliffs. 'Pierced Form (Epidauros)' (1960) is one of the carvings of African wood (the latest of which were made in 1963), and comparable to 'Corinthos' for the relation between the white-painted interior and the polished, wooden skin. 'Figure (Nyanga)' (1959–60) is remarkable for its broad proportions, and its shape is markedly affected by the spectacular graining of the elm.

There are three sculptures in the collection (one in two versions) that were maquettes commissioned for large works for specific public sites. In each case the building they were to adorn was already complete, or nearly so, but in only one of these had the architect planned in the first place to include sculpture. This is the earliest of the three, 'Garden Sculpture (Model for Meridian)' (1958), which is in the style of her earliest bronzes based on the shape of bent metal. The architect of State House, High Holborn, had authority to plan the sculpture directly with the artist, who first visited the site during the early stages of construction. The five foot model at St Ives is identical in configuration to the final fifteen foot bronze, but has a much rougher surface. Such close cooperation between patron and artist was unusual, and for the commission from the John Lewis Partnership for a lightweight sculpture high on the side wall of their just completed Oxford Street store, Barbara Hepworth sent the brass 'Maquette, Three Forms in Echelon' (1961) to London for approval. This model was rejected, and the sculpture eventually installed in 1963 was an enlargement in aluminium of 'Winged Figure' (1957). Another version of the 'Maquette' was cast in bronze in 1965.

The carving in walnut 'Single Form (September)' (1961) is both an idea for a large sculpture for the forecourt of the United Nations skyscraper in New York and a finished work on its own. It was made before she officially received the commission but after she had talked about it with the Secretary-General, Dag Hammarskjold, who was a collector of her work and a personal friend. The complicated patterns on the surface of the walnut evidently influenced the particular shape of the outline. Barbara Hepworth subtitled the carving 'September' after Hammarskjold's accidental death in September 1961. His wishes were eventually put into effect, and the huge twenty-one foot high bronze 'Single Form', cast in several pieces, was unveiled in New York in June 1964. At the ceremony the artist spoke of the sculpture as a memorial to Dag Hammarskjold and as a symbol of his ideas. The monument recalls the shapes of her abstract sculptures of the 1930s, such as one of the 'Forms in Echelon' (1938). The contrast between the small, avant-garde wood carving exhibited in London at the Guggenheim Jeune Gallery in 1939 and the huge bronze at one of the most critical sites in the world twenty-five years later is as remarkable as is the continuity of style. The moral dimensions were present from the beginning, and Hepworth had written in *Circle* in 1937 of her simplified, abstract sculpture as a hope for social and individual freedom. The change in scale, material and design of the two variations of the same idea were manipulated by the artist in a way comparable to the change of expression in a face by the alteration of parts within the same design. Barbara Hepworth recorded in 1960 that she now found the 'placid academic recognition' of abstract art 'disconcerting', and her success must ironically have given the problem of restoring the cutting edge of surprise to her work. To Hammarskjold, however, also of Hepworth's generation, the pre-war idealism of aesthetic democracy was implied by such abstract art.

IV

There are few works by Barbara Hepworth in the Tate Gallery collection from the years 1965–7, and there was a reduction in her activity during this time as she was seriously ill. The large 'Construction (Crucifixion)' (1966), unusual in her work and made of painted bronze cast from welded metal, was associated with this, as was a series of small maquettes intended to be made later. It is remarkable that the work from the last ten years of her life, after this pause, constitutes a 'late style', which, although she had been gradually working towards it, can be considered as a distinct and final episode of her career. The sculptures are characterised by a much freer and less abstract link between their appearance and their mood. Her own description in 1969/70 of her work after 1960 is relevant: '. . . emergence of subconscious imagery, and a general fusion of ideas and themes.'

'Two Figures (Menhirs)' of 1964 leads towards the style of the last sculptures. The title refers to both the ancient monuments of Cornwall – the standing stones, relics of a forgotten religion and yet still a disturbing emotional presence – and also to figures, and the apertures in the sculpture resemble watching eyes. This physiognomic association is much more powerful in this case than it is, for example, in the superficially similar 'Forms in Echelon' (1938). The material, two large pieces of slate, is unusual and particularly rich in colour. These features, strong natural colour and a highly polished and impersonal surface, along with the suggestion of mystery, are typical of the works of this last period.

Barbara Hepworth was now able to rely on the experience of three assistants who had been with her a long time, and who were craftsmen rather than artists. She did little work in wood, and the shapes of work in various marbles, slate and bronze came to look like one another, as the material was selected for its colour rather than its instrinsic quality. Many of the titles refer to magic, and in a recorded conversation of 1970 she mentioned both the prehistoric 'Men-an-Tol' stones and the Goonhilly Downs tracking station as comparisons. Their significance is not only their frightening presence, but also their essential association with the landscape.

'Two Forms (Divided Circle)' (1969) is of necessity made of bronze because of its large size and the extraordinary playing with unbalance: having been concerned all her life to make her sculptures stand properly Barbara Hepworth in contrast splits a stable shape in such a way to give immense tension in the base, and the forms look as if arrested in the moment of falling. The size invites one to stand between the two halves: with little restriction on size she was now able to fulfil her ambition of placing the sculpture right around the viewer, as if their roles were reversed. The impression that the sculpture is a large face is unavoidable. The concave surfaces of the holes are patinated a different colour to the smooth exterior of the bronze, and shaped and marked similarly to the carved holes of, for example, the African wood sculptures.

'Touchstone' (1969), 'Oval with Two Forms' (1971) and 'Rock Face' (1973) are all highly polished so as to reveal the colour of the material, played on particularly in 'Oval with Two Forms' in the contrast between the three different materials (unlike the sculptures with separate parts of the 1930s, where the material of each was always the same). The title 'Touchstone' implies that the stone itself has magic powers and is a test of value, and at the same time means that it should be fingered. 'Rock Face' is similarly ambiguous, and it is uncertain whether it is the sculpture or the viewer that is intended to be the more actively looking. This two-way relation with the sculptures as seen and felt is important to Barbara Hepworth's feeling that they were objects in a landscape, separate from her but nevertheless in the landscape which she shared. The precision of their carving suggests contemporary technology, particularly in 'Rock

Face' with its overall rectangular shape, in contrast to the organic shapes she had mostly used previously.

The position of the black and white stones within 'Oval with Two Forms' is fixed, but their size suggests, like the figures of 'Group I (Concourse) February 4 1951', that they have been arranged intuitively. The earlier 'Six Forms (2 × 3)' (1963) implies much freer rearrangement. Barbara Hepworth often piled shapes into two or three storeys at this time, but the title states that the forms themselves were each separate. There are other sculptures of 1967–8, on both a small and a very large scale, that are made of similar elements. Such multi-part sculpture developed into her last major works, four sculptures of groups, two of white marble and two of bronze. The marble 'Fallen Images' (1974) at St Ives is the latest of these and her last sculpture. It is connected closely to the other marble group 'Assembly of Sea Forms' (1972), which is also on a low, cylindrical turntable. The turntable itself symbolised for Barbara Hepworth the turning of the earth and the erosion caused by time:

> 'We are so placed here, geographically, that both sun and moon rise and set over the water with a great radiance and this fact sets up a remarkable tension in my everyday life. I am not scientifically minded; but the forces between the everchanging position of the sun and moon, and the effects upon sea and tide, and cloud and wind, which change the depth of shadow on forms have governed my life for a long time.
>
> I began to get more and more turn-tables and to try to assess my own changing movements in relation to the sun.' (1970, A Pictorial Autobiography)

The eight separate parts of 'Assembly of Sea Forms' are individually named, some as members of a family, some as seashore objects. Similarly the tallest forms of 'Fallen Images' suggest man and woman. The coastal associations remain, as does the suggestion yet again of both Cornish menhirs and the Goonhilly Downs tracking station. For her last work Barbara Hepworth went back again to the various 'Three Forms' of 1934–5, but in spite of the greater geometrical precision of the later and much larger group the symbolism is more open and wider ranging: based on the idea of the family and of Cornwall it extends to the technological and cosmic.

Short Bibliography

STATEMENTS BY THE ARTIST

In *Unit One: The Modern Movement in English Architecture, Painting and Sculpture*, Herbert Read, editor Cassell, London, 1934
'Sculpture', in *Circle: International Survey of Constructive Art*, J.L. Martin, Ben Nicholson and Naum Gabo editors, Faber and Faber, London, 1937
In *Barbara Hepworth. Carvings and Drawings*, Introduction by Herbert Read, Lund Humphries & Co. Ltd, London, 1952
Edouard Roditi, *Dialogues on Art*, Secker and Warburg, London, 1960
Barbara Hepworth, *A Pictorial Autobiography*, Adams and Dart, Bath, 1970

CATALOGUES

The Sculpture is catalogued in two volumes, with a third to follow
J.P. Hodin, *Barbara Hepworth*, Lund Humphries, London, 1961
Alan Bowness, *The Complete Sculpture of Barbara Hepworth 1960–69* Lund Humphries, London, 1971

MONOGRAPHS AND BOOKLETS

William Gibson, *Barbara Hepworth*, Faber and Faber, London, 1946
Michael Shepherd, *Barbara Hepworth*, Methuen, London, 1963
A.M. Hammacher, *Barbara Hepworth*, Thames & Hudson, London, 1968
Alan Bowness, *Barbara Hepworth, Drawings from a Sculptor's Landscape*, Cory Adams and Mackay, London, 1966

EXHIBITION CATALOGUES

Barbara Hepworth, Retrospective Exhibition, 1927–1954, Whitechapel Art Gallery, 1954 Introduction by David Baxandall
Barbara Hepworth, An exhibition of Sculpture from 1952–1962, Whitechapel Art Gallery, 1962 Introduction by Bryan Robertson
Barbara Hepworth, Tate Gallery, 1968. Introduction by Ronald Alley
Barbara Hepworth, City Art Gallery, Plymouth, 1970. Introduction by Edwin Mullins
Barbara Hepworth, Late Works, Edinburgh International Festival, 1976. Introduction by Douglas Hall

Detailed catalogue information on the Tate Gallery's collection of Barbara Hepworth is available in *The Modern British paintings, drawings and sculpture*, vol. I, 1964, and, for works acquired later, in the relevant volume of the *Biennial Report* or (from 1974–6) *Illustrated Catalogue of Acquisitions*.

Illustrated catalogue

Works at St Ives are marked □

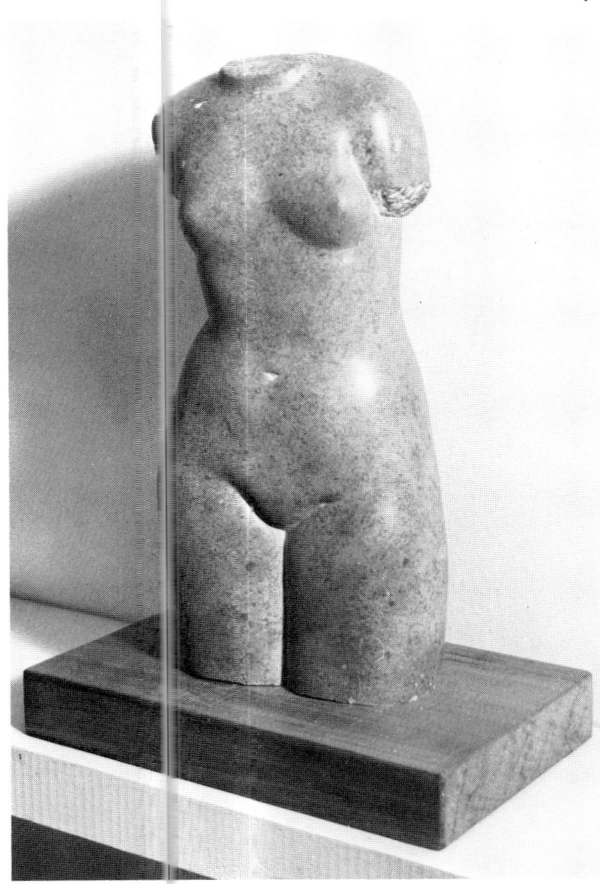

□ **Torso** 1923

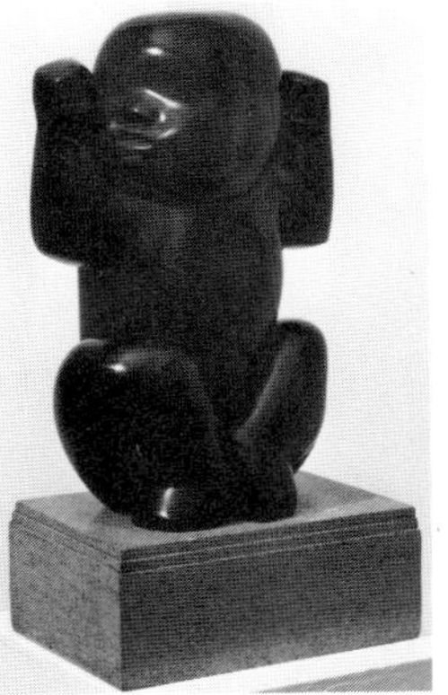

□ **Infant** 1929

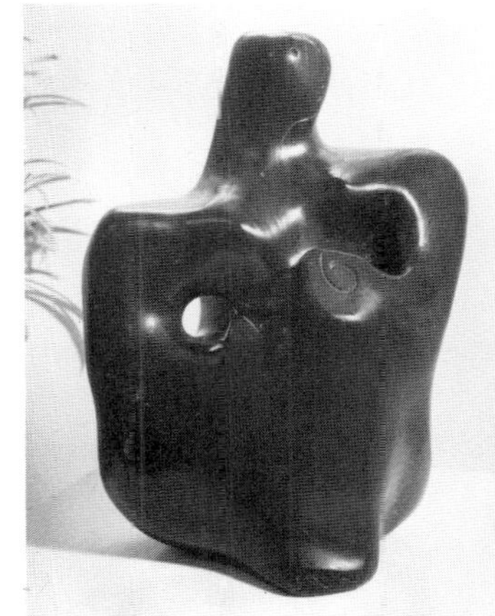

□ **Seated Figure** 1932–3

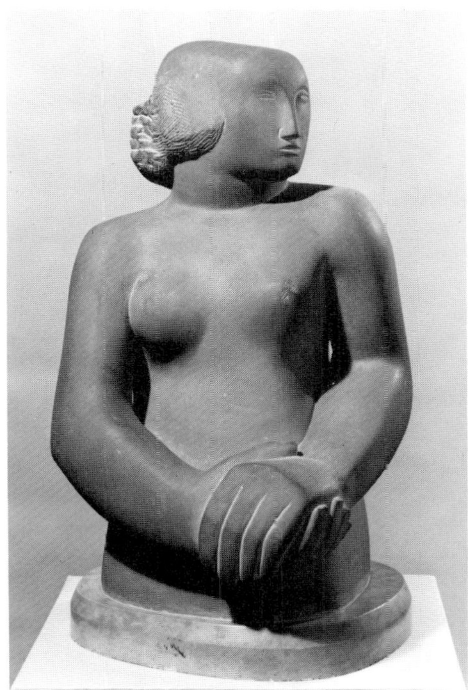

Figure of a Woman 1929–30

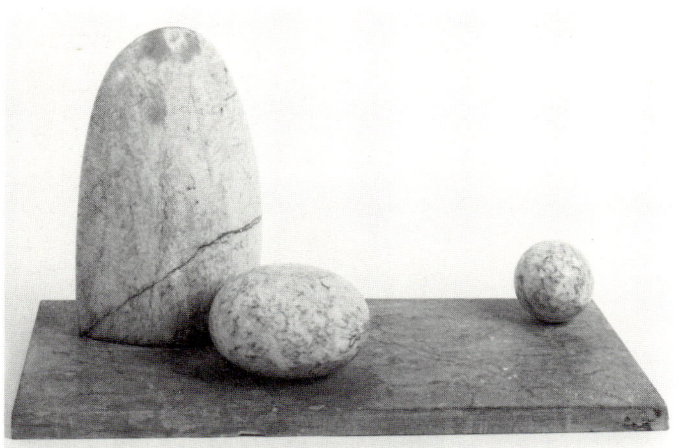

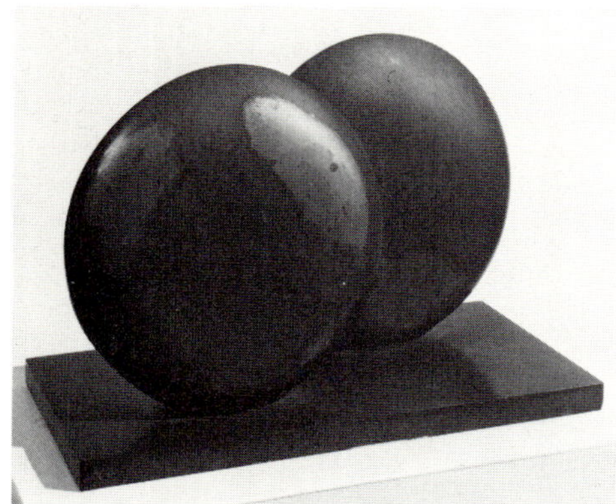

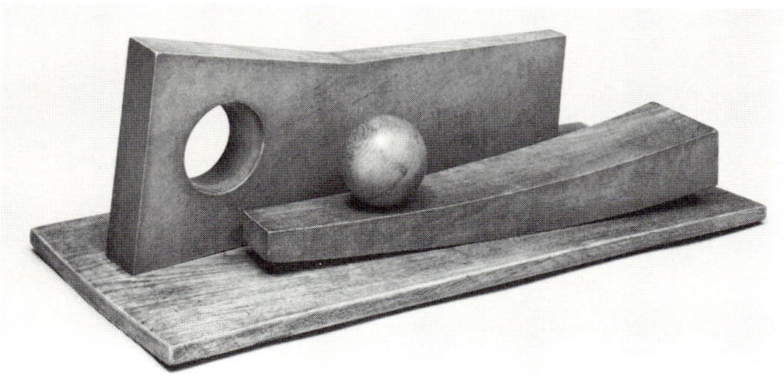

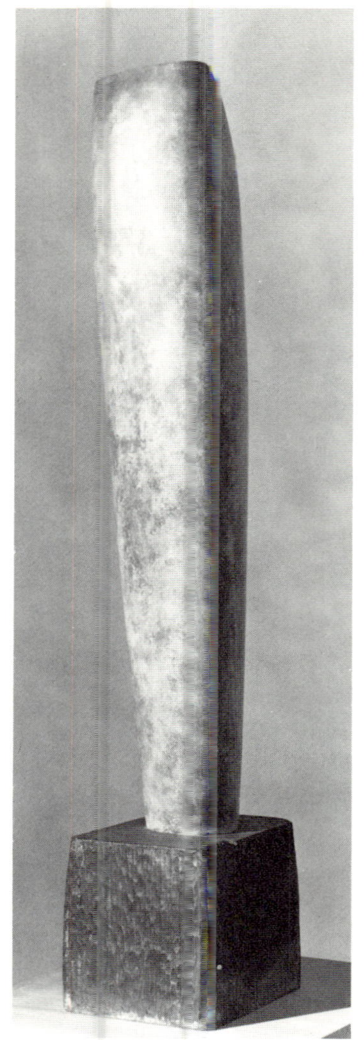

Single Form (Eikon) 1937–8

above left
□ **Three Forms** 1934

above centre
□ **Discs in Echelon** 1935

left
Ball, Plane and Hole 1936

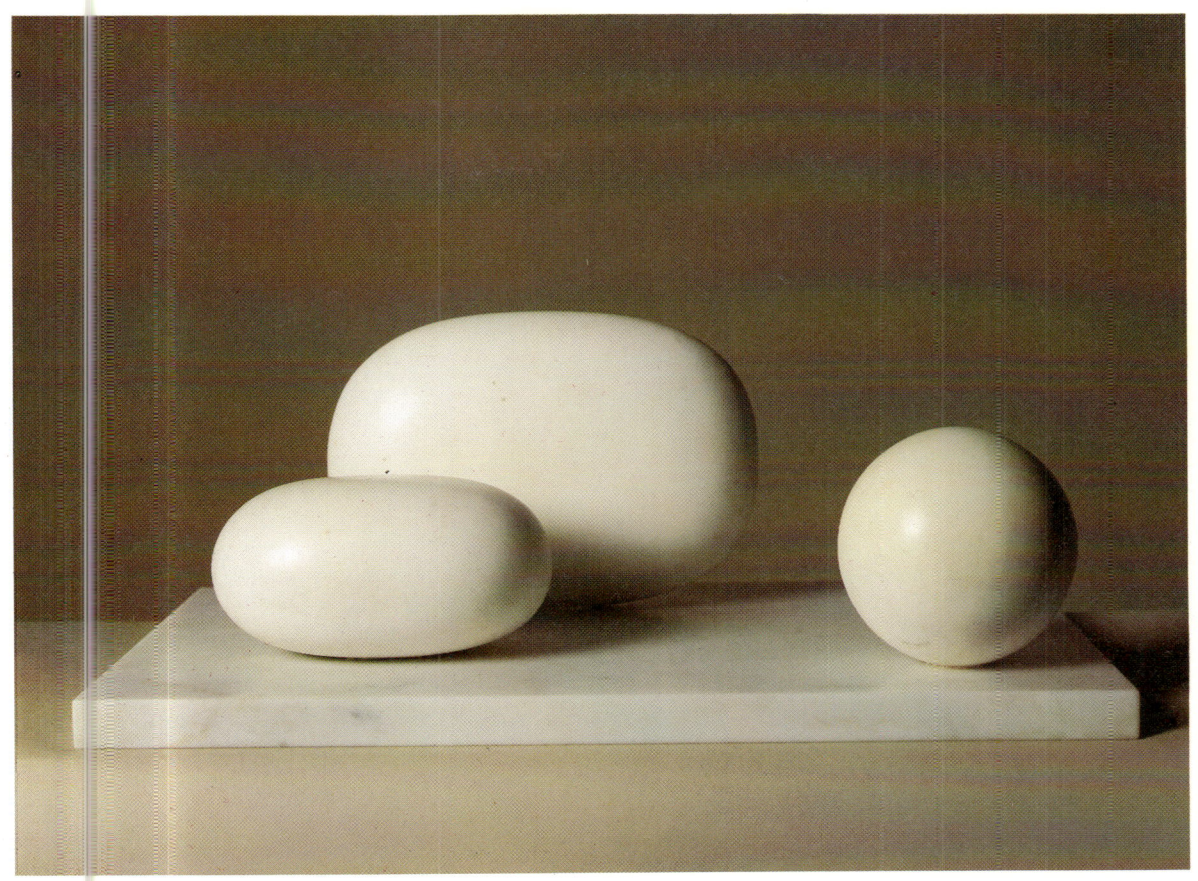

Three Forms 1935

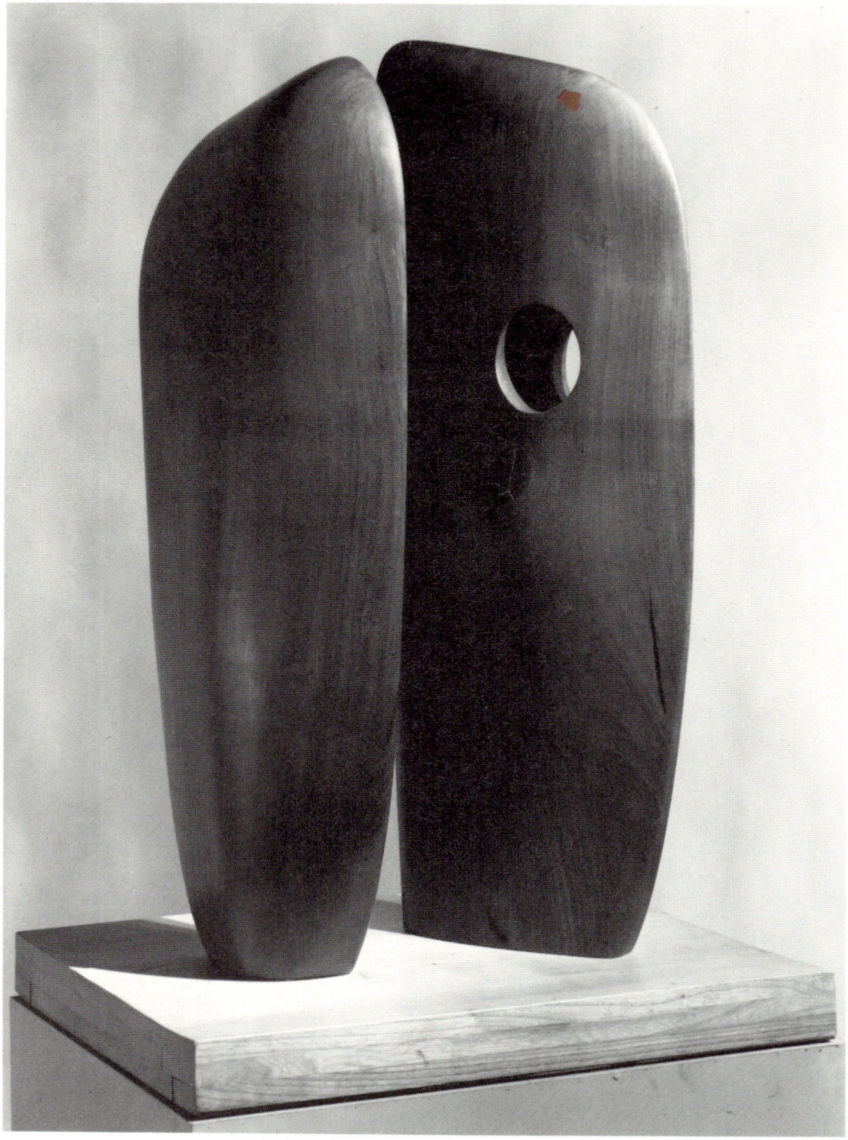

Forms in Echelon 1938

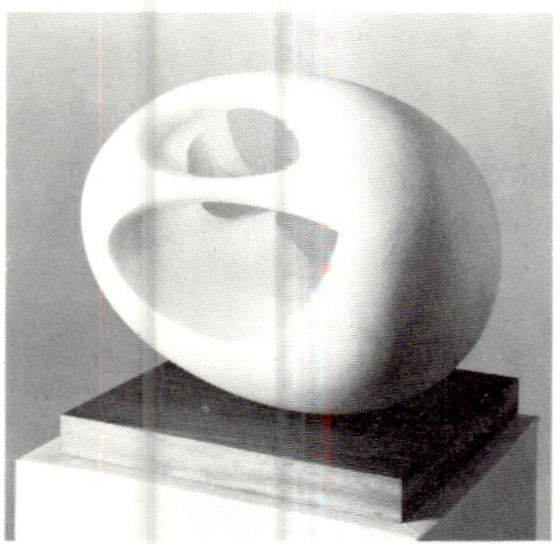

Oval Sculpture (No.2) 1943

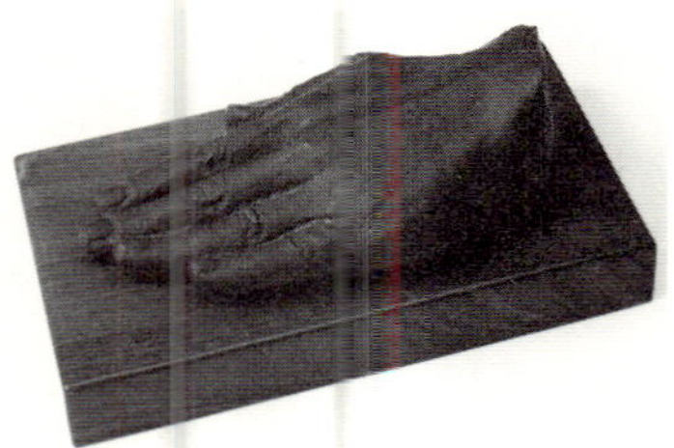

□ **The Artist's Hand** 1943–4

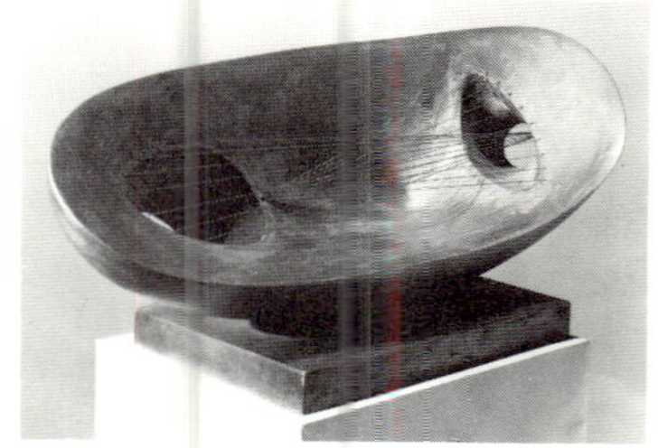

Landscape Sculpture 1944

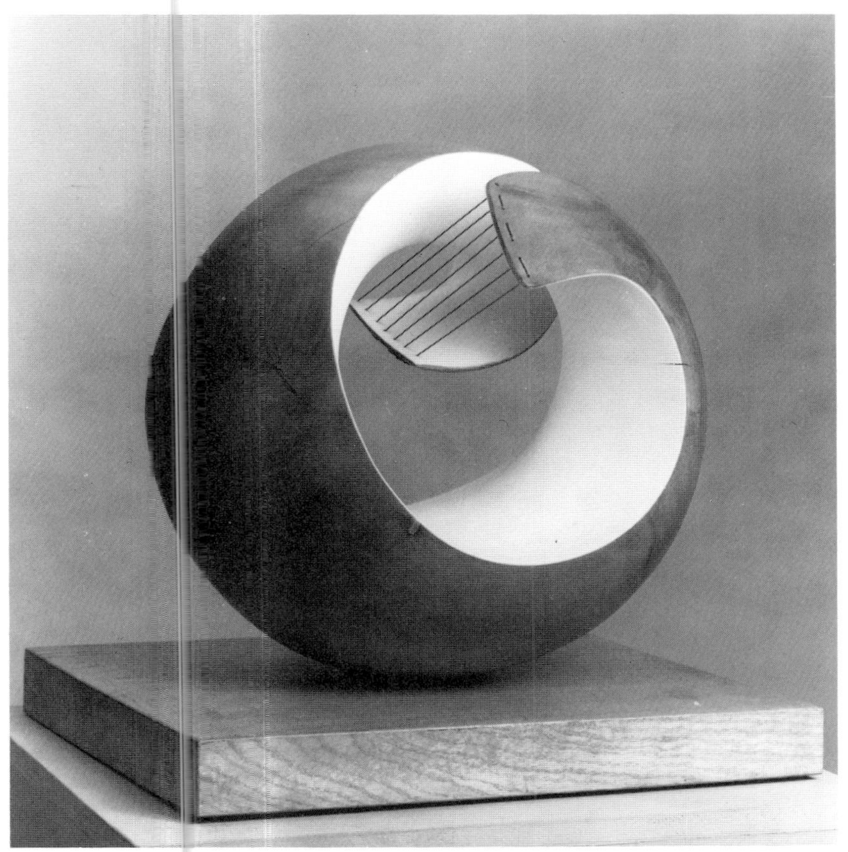

Pelagos 1946

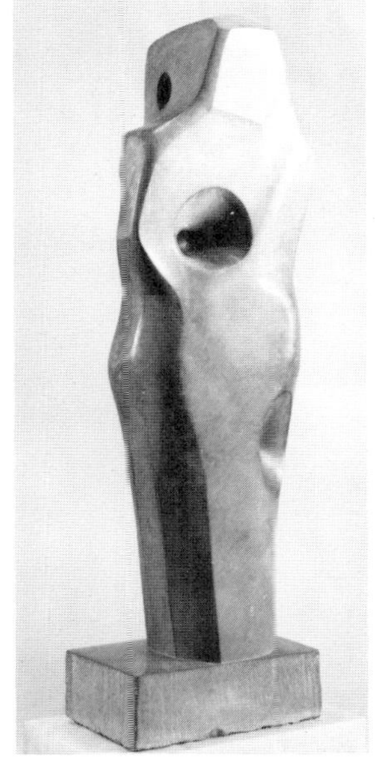

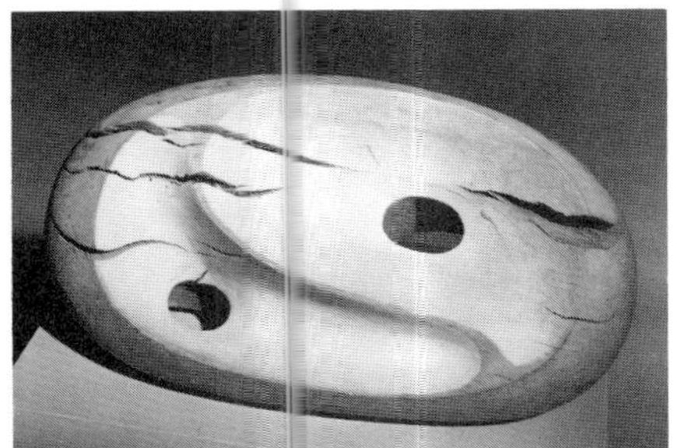

Tides I 1946

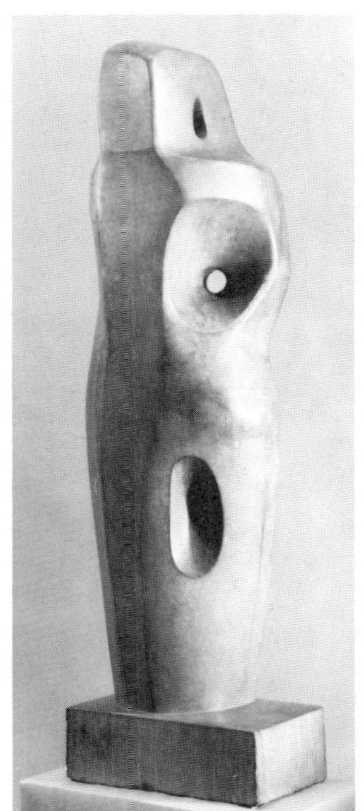

above + right
Bicentric Form 1949

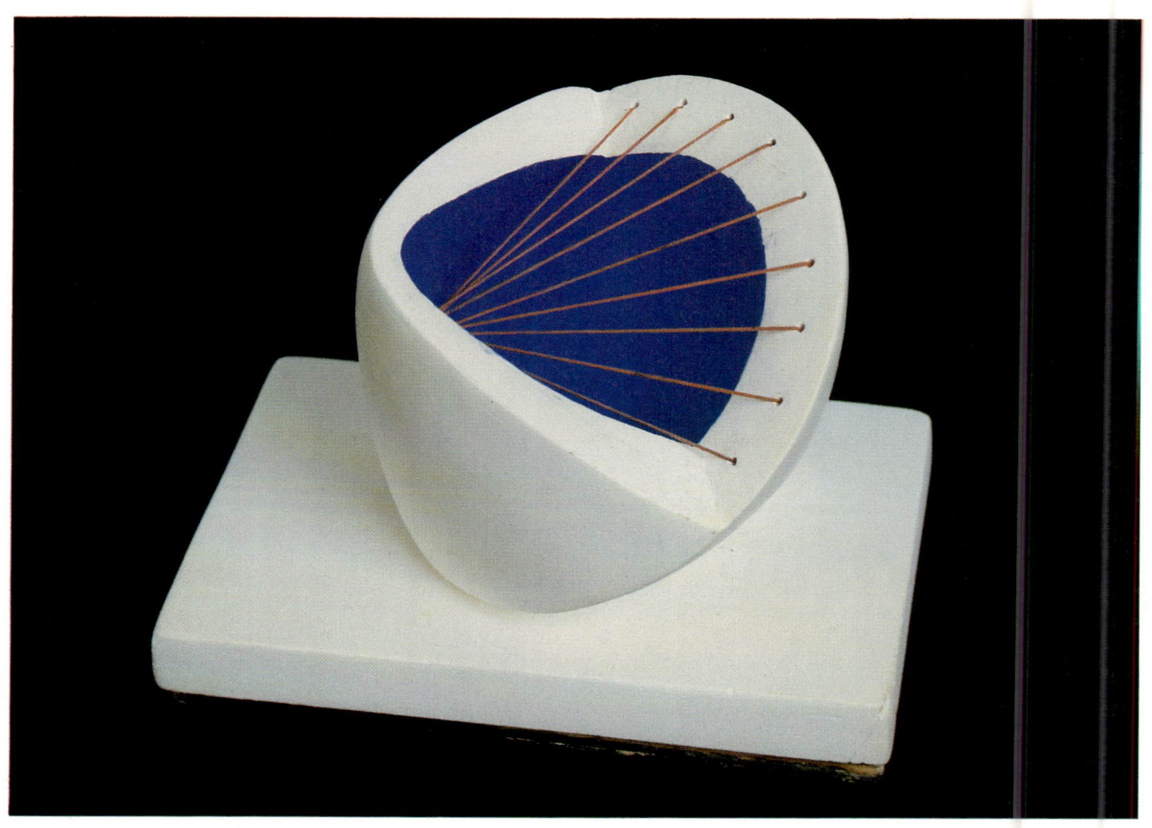

□ **Sculpture with Colour, Deep Blue and Red** 1940

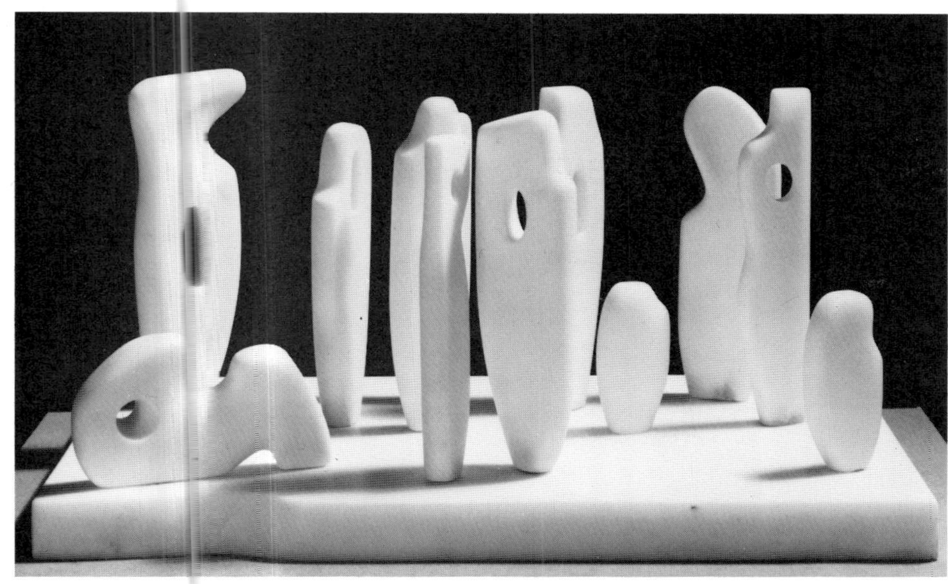

left
Group I (Concourse), February 4 1951 1951

below left
Corinthos 1954–5

below centre
□ **Coré** 1955–6

below right
□ **Poised Form** 1951–2

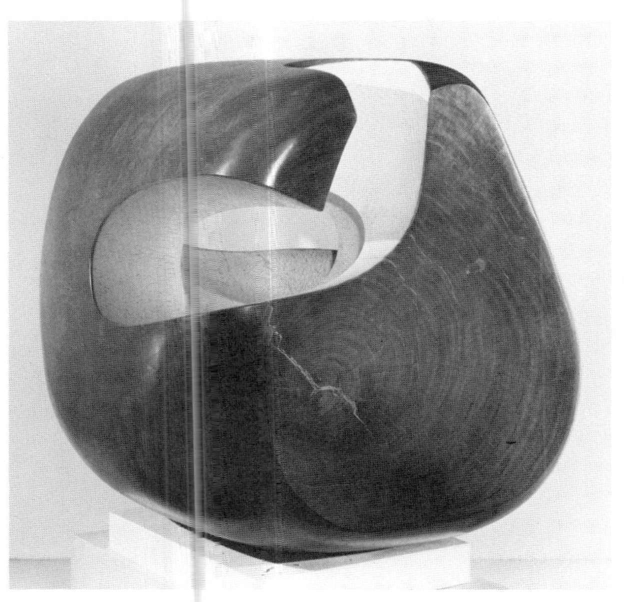

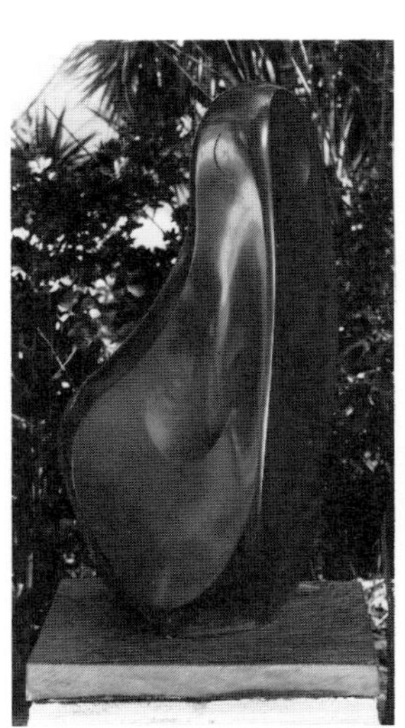

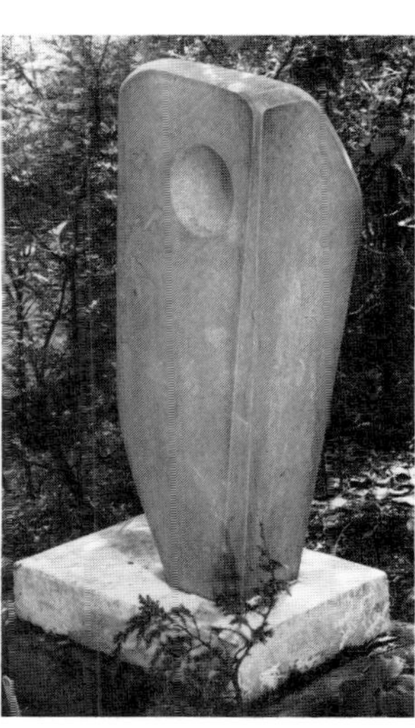

left
□ **Forms in Movement (Pavan)** 1956
below left
Curved Form (Travalgan) 1956
below
Orpheus (Maquette 2, version I) 1956

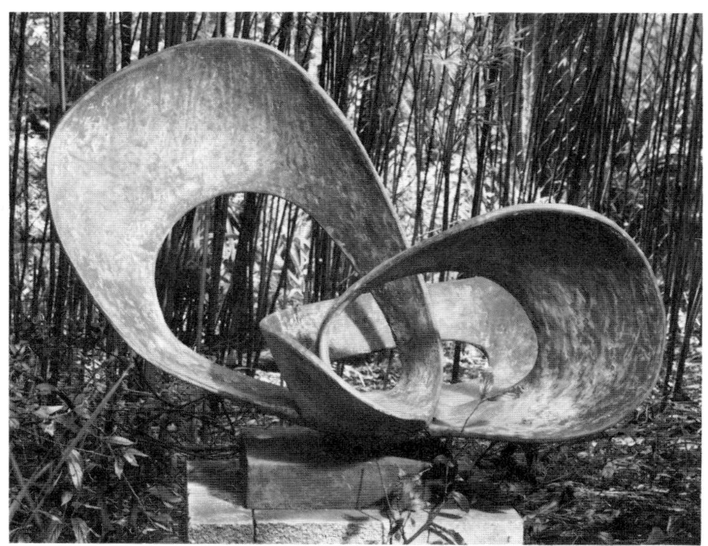

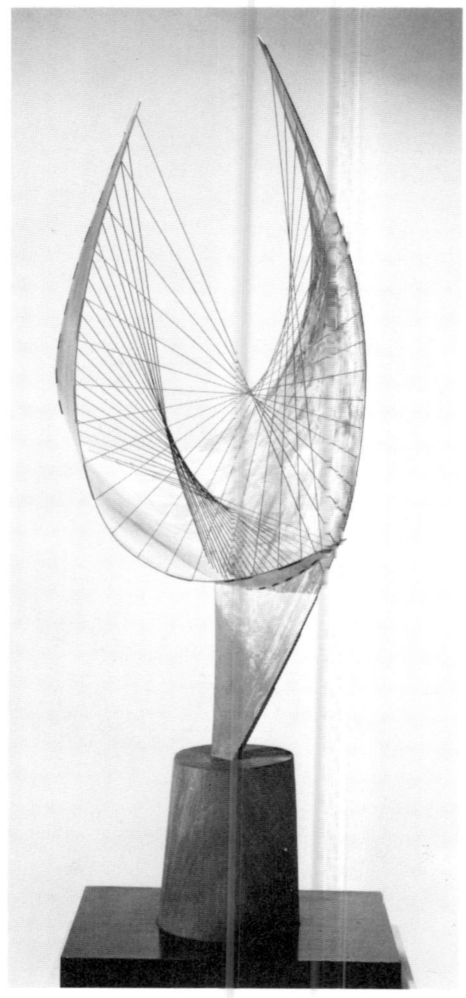

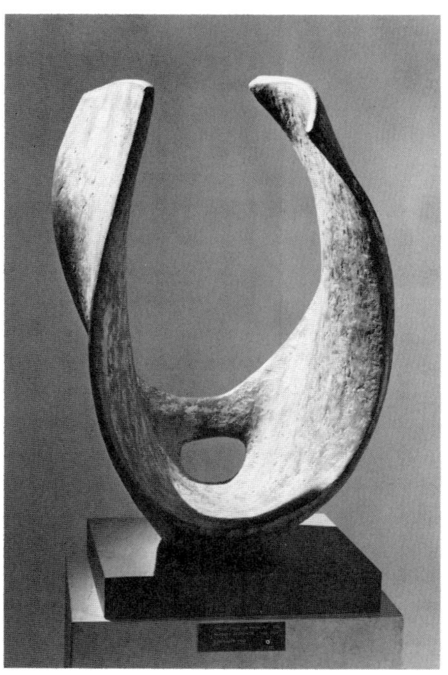

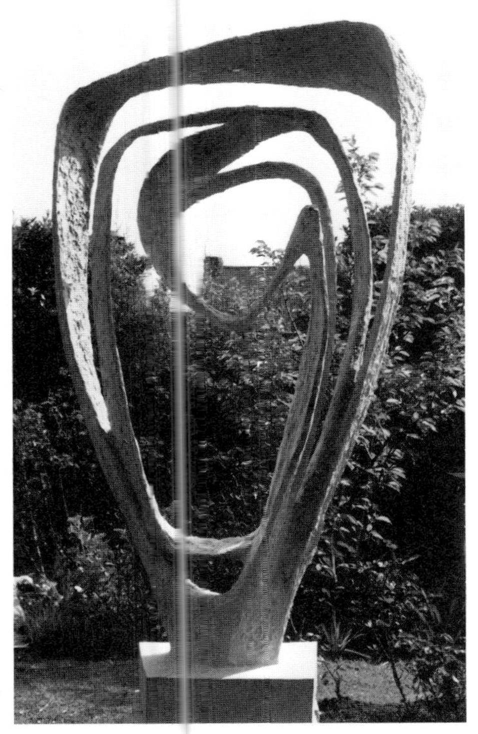

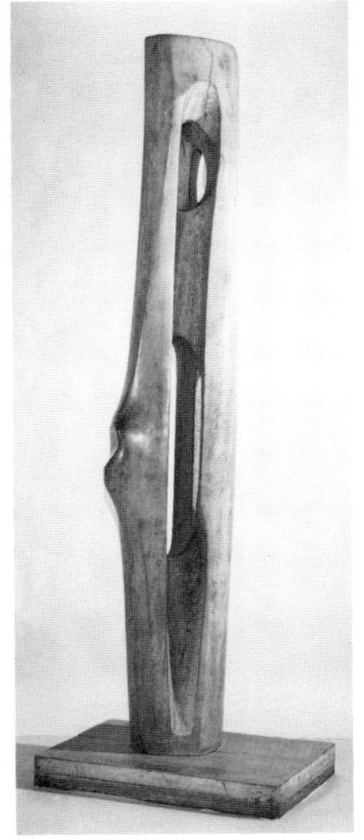

Figure (Nanjizal) 1958

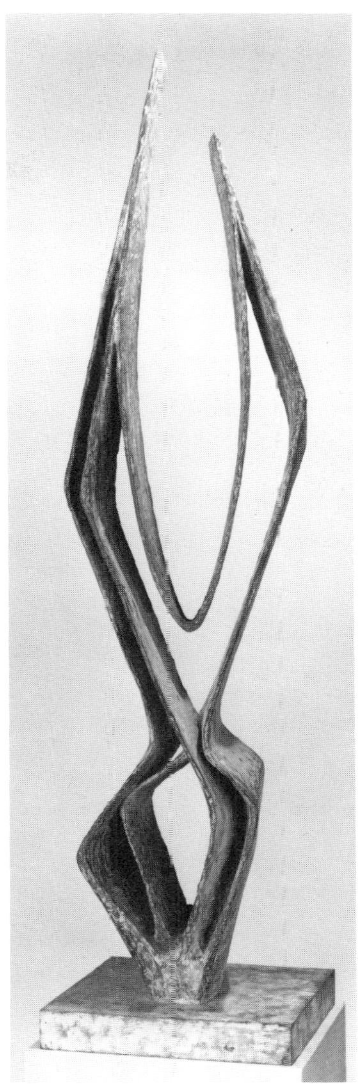

Cantate Domino 1958

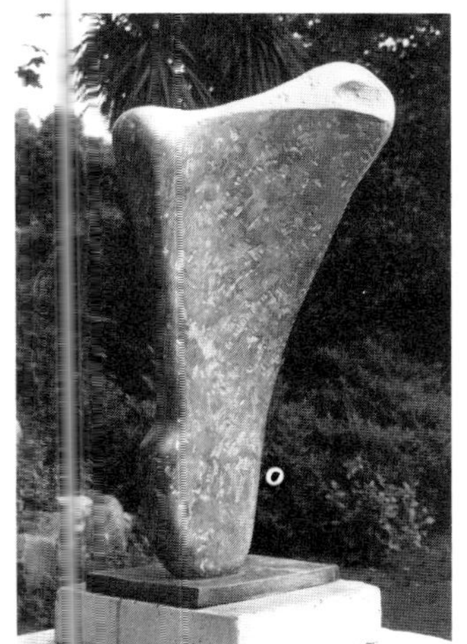

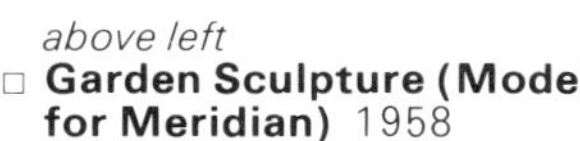

above left
□ **Garden Sculpture (Model for Meridian)** 1958

left
□ **Torso II (Torcello)** 1958

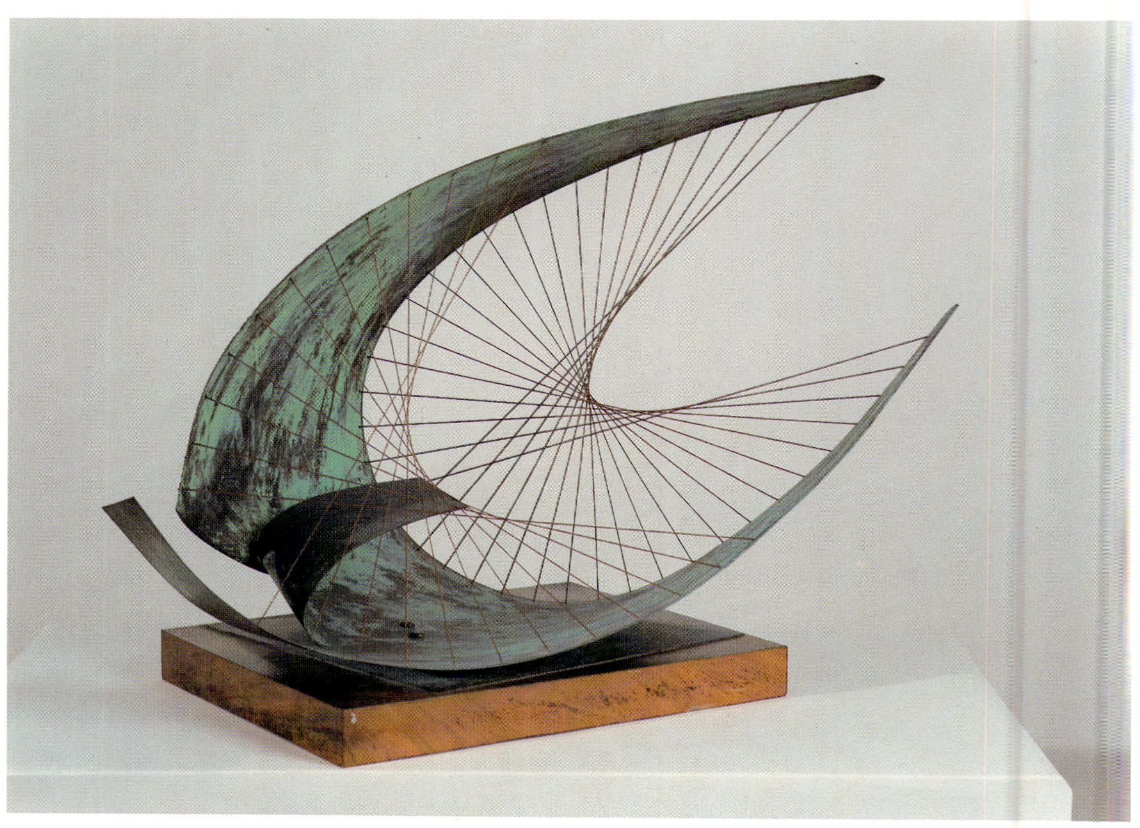

□ **Stringed Figure (Curlew), version II** 1956

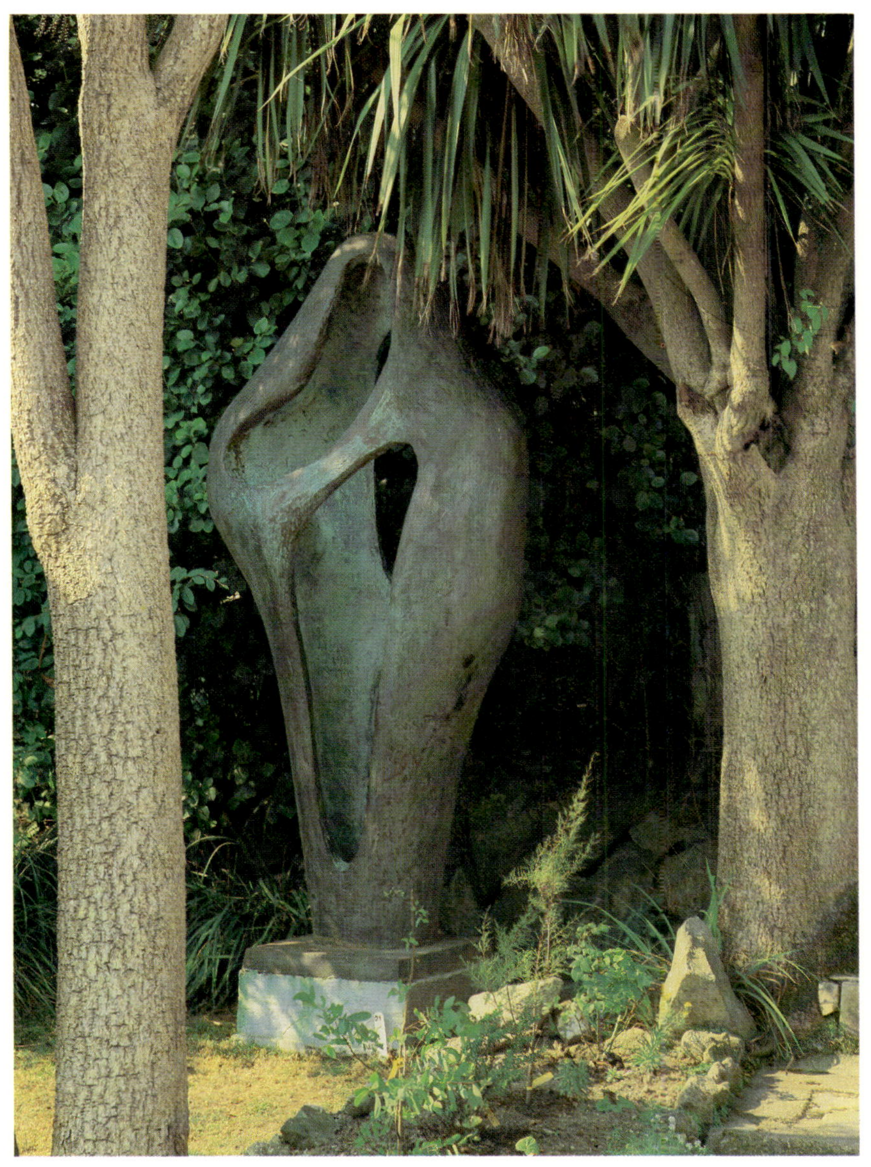

□ **Figure for Landscape** 1960

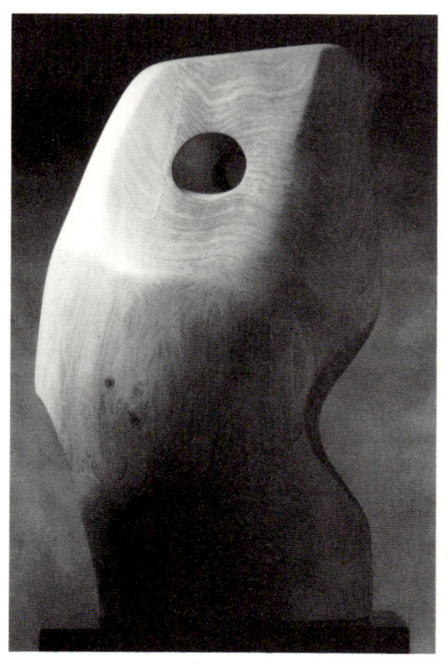

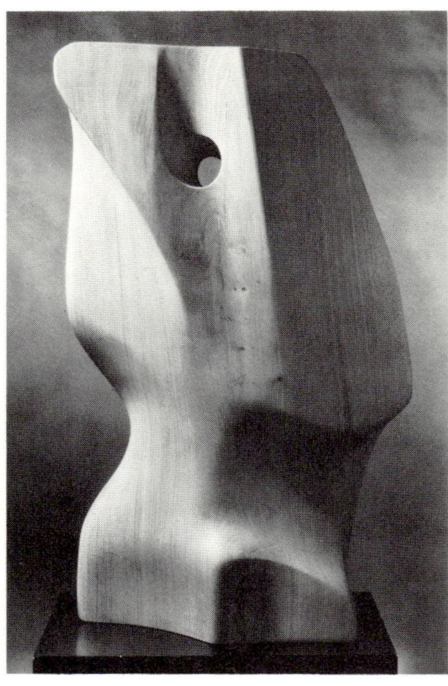

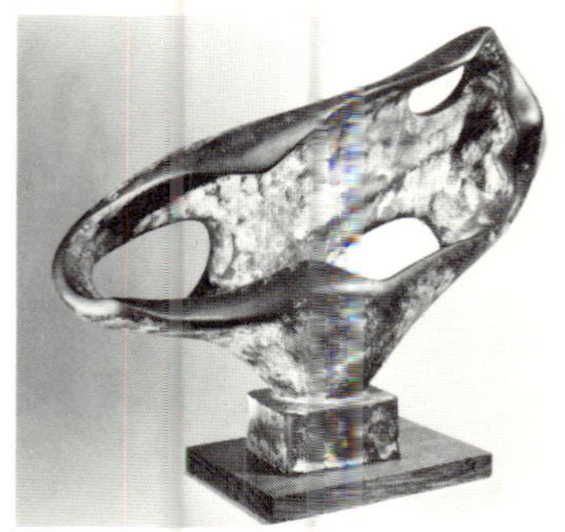

above
Sea Form (Porthmeor) 1958

left + centre
Figure (Nyanga) 1959–60

below left
Image II 1960

below right
□ **Pierced Form (Epidauros)** 1960

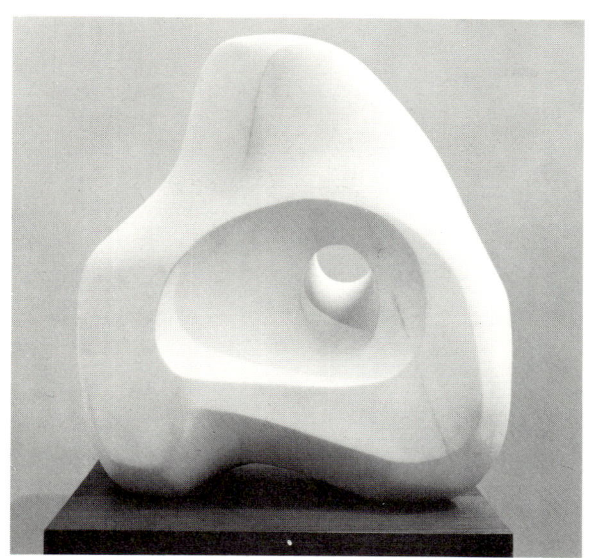

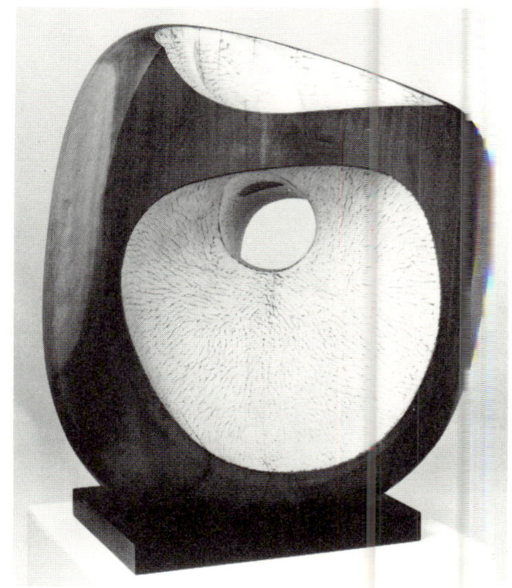

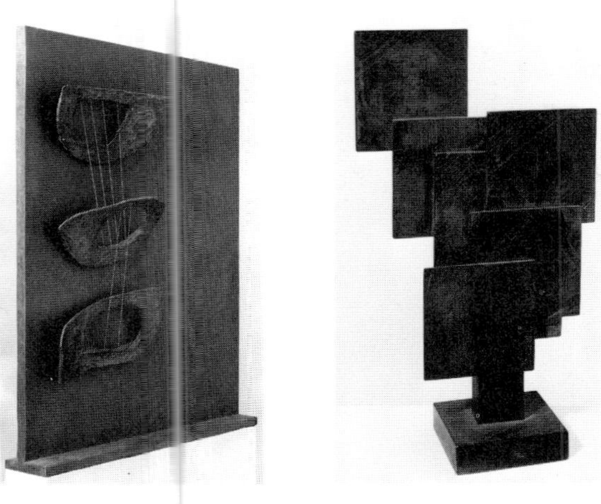

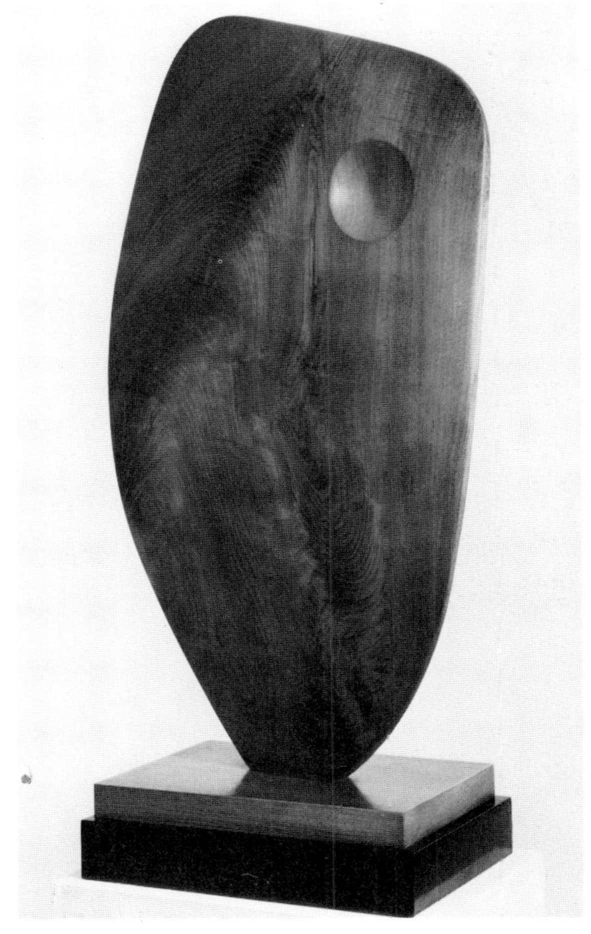

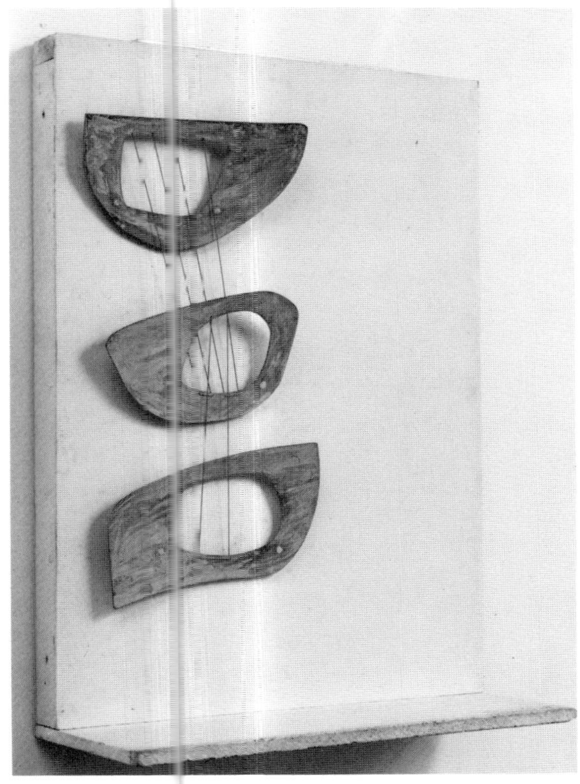

above
□ **Single Form (September)** 1961

above centre
□ **Square Forms** 1962

above left
Maquette, Three Forms in Echelon 1961

left
□ **Maquette, Three Forms in Echelon** 1961

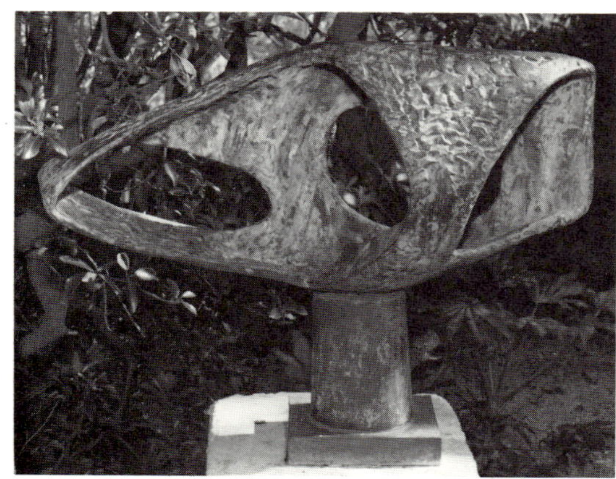

□ **Bronze Form (Patmos)** 1962–3

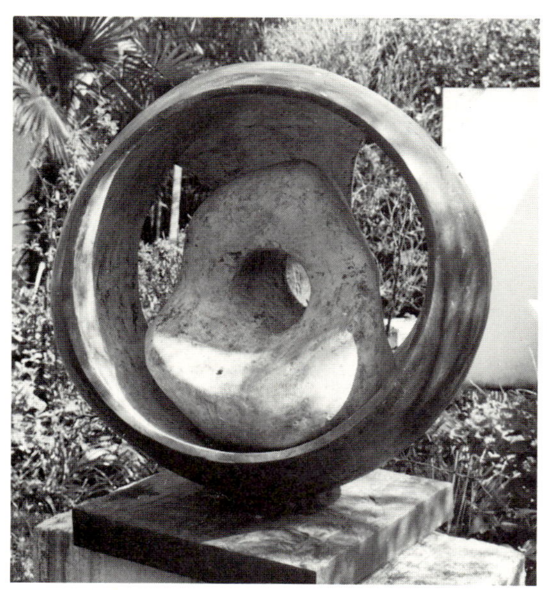

□ **Sphere with Inner Form** 1963

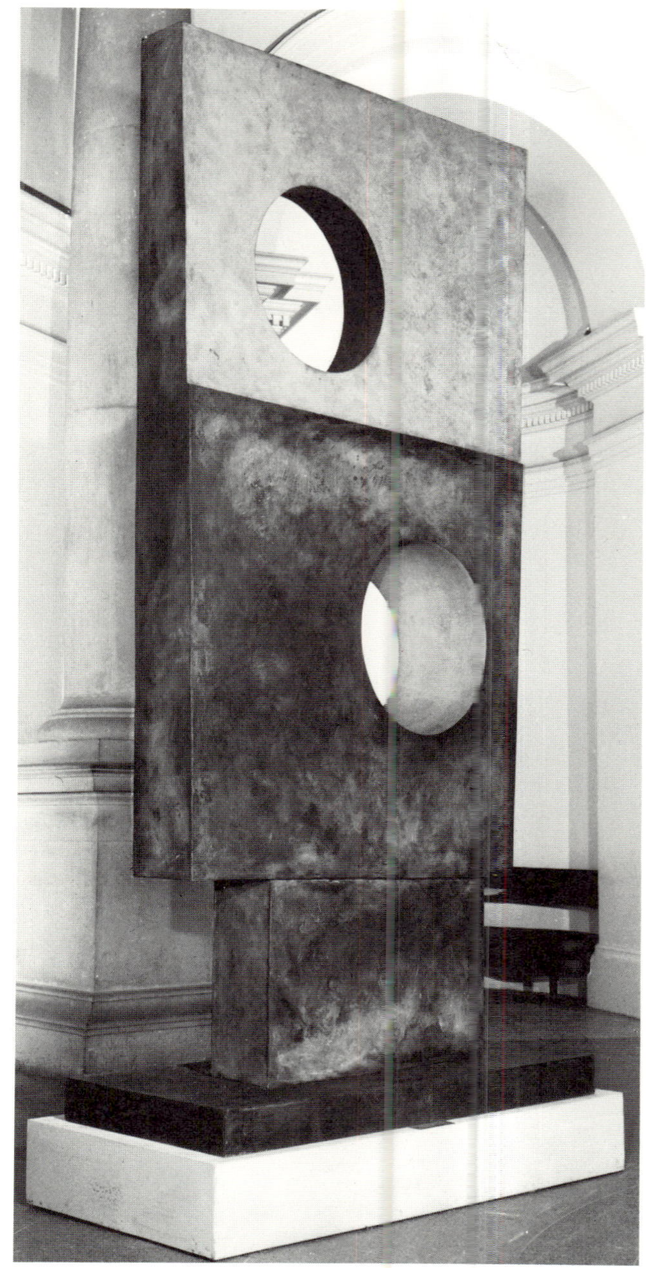

Squares with Two Circles 1963

Two Figures (Menhirs) 1964

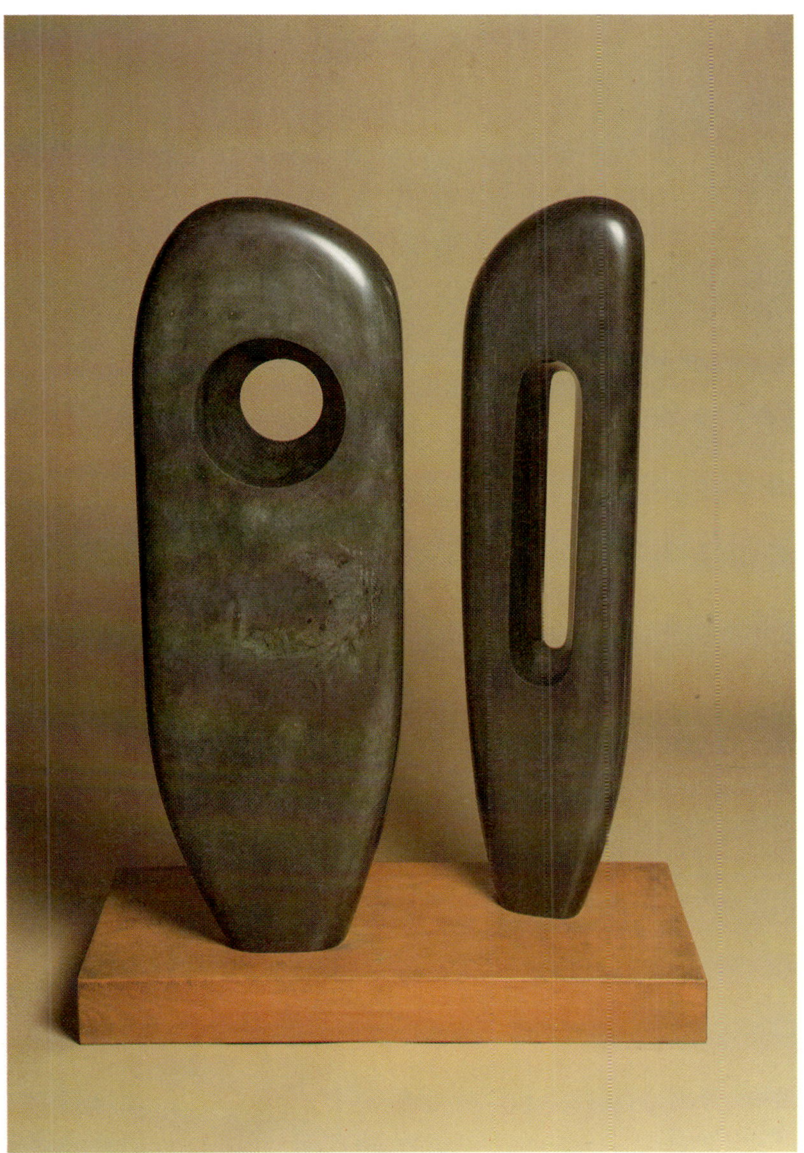

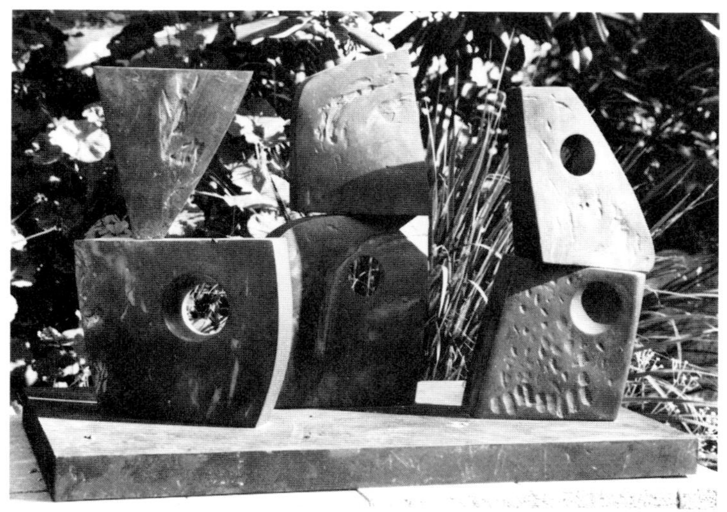

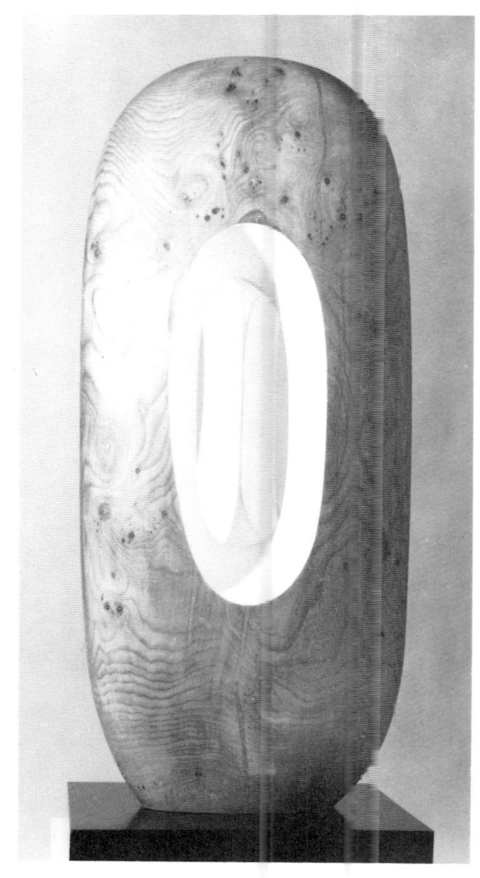

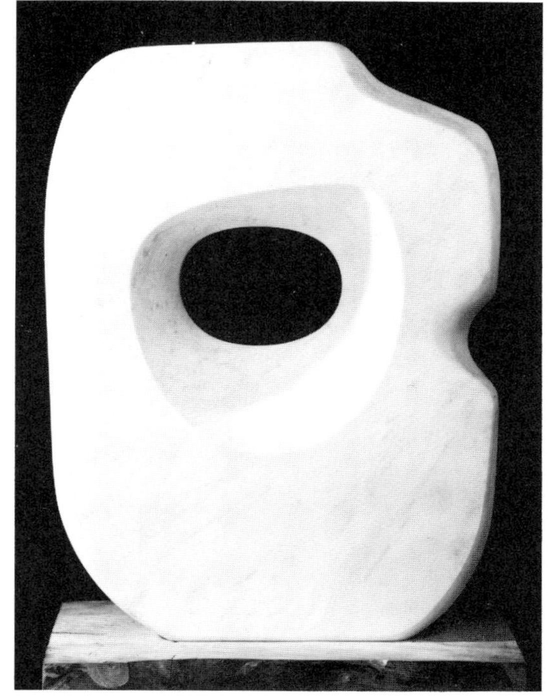

above left
□ **Six Forms (2 × 3)** 1968

above
Hollow Form with White (Elegy III) 1965

left
Pierced Form 1963–4

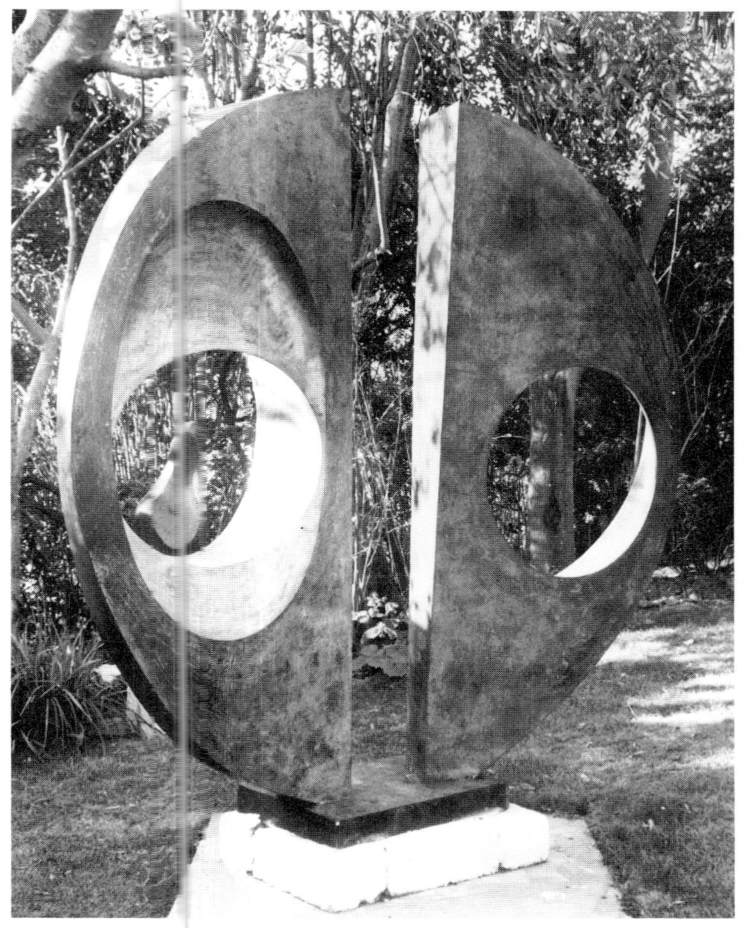

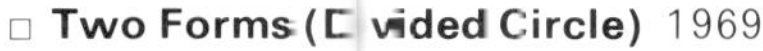

□ **Two Forms (Divided Circle)** 1969

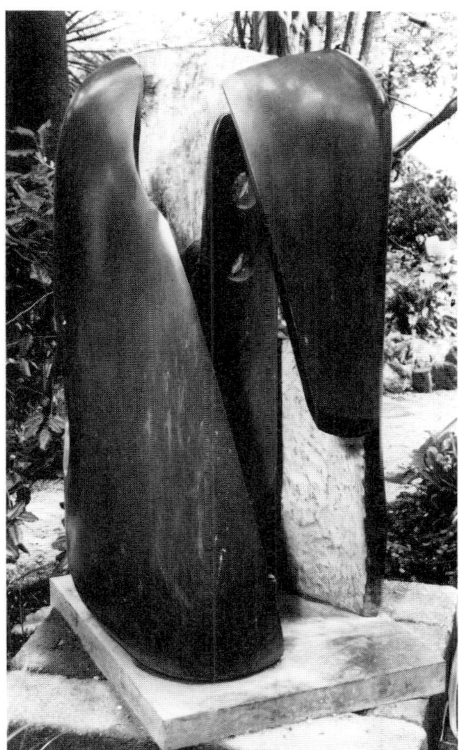

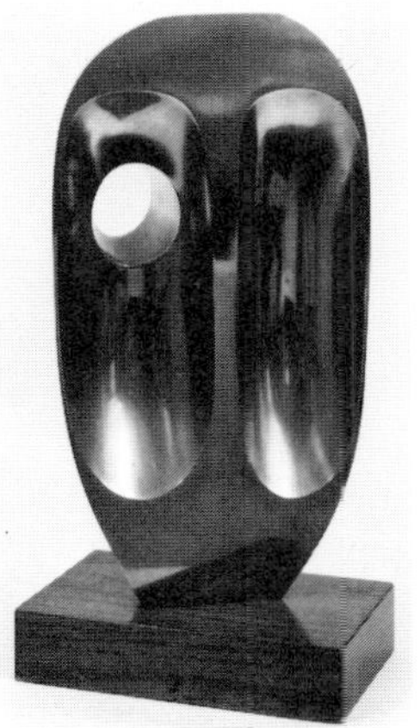

above right
□ **Hollow Form with Inner Form** 1968

right
□ **Vertical Form (St Ives)** 1968

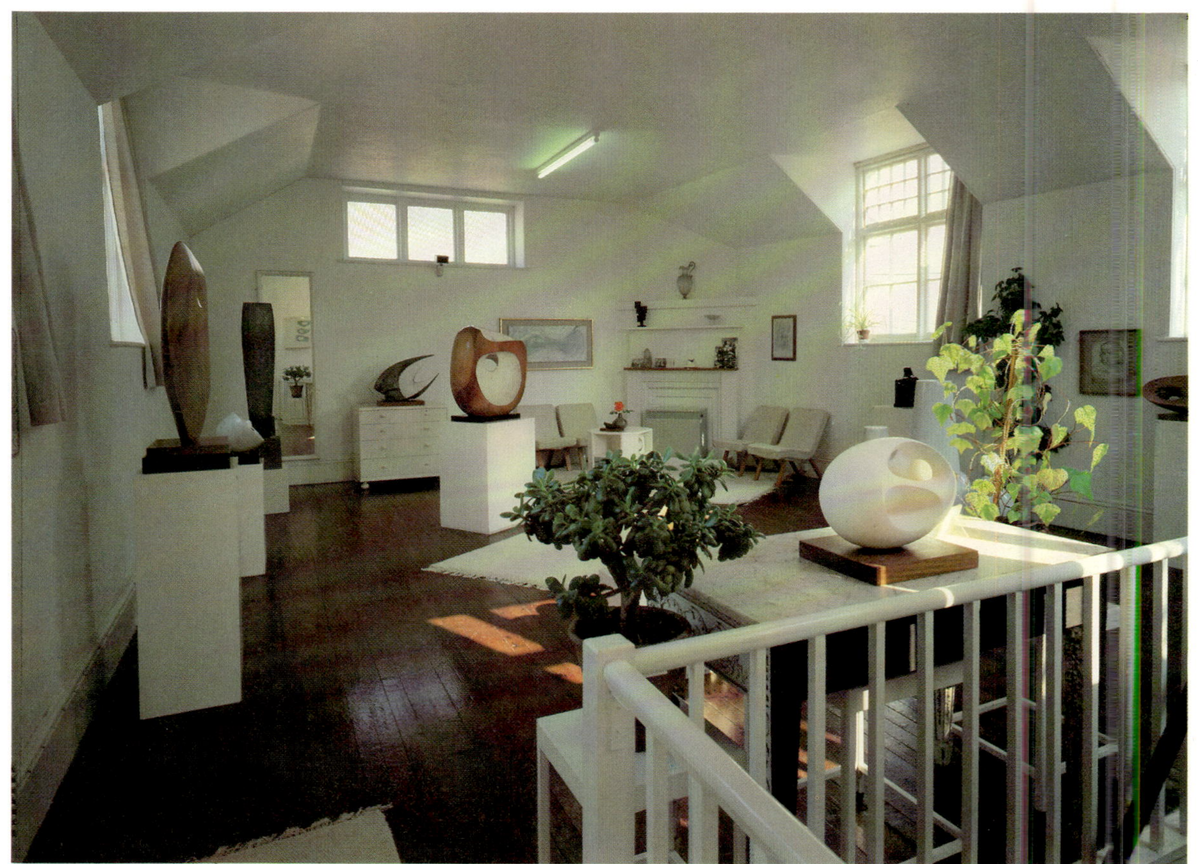

View of the studio, St Ives

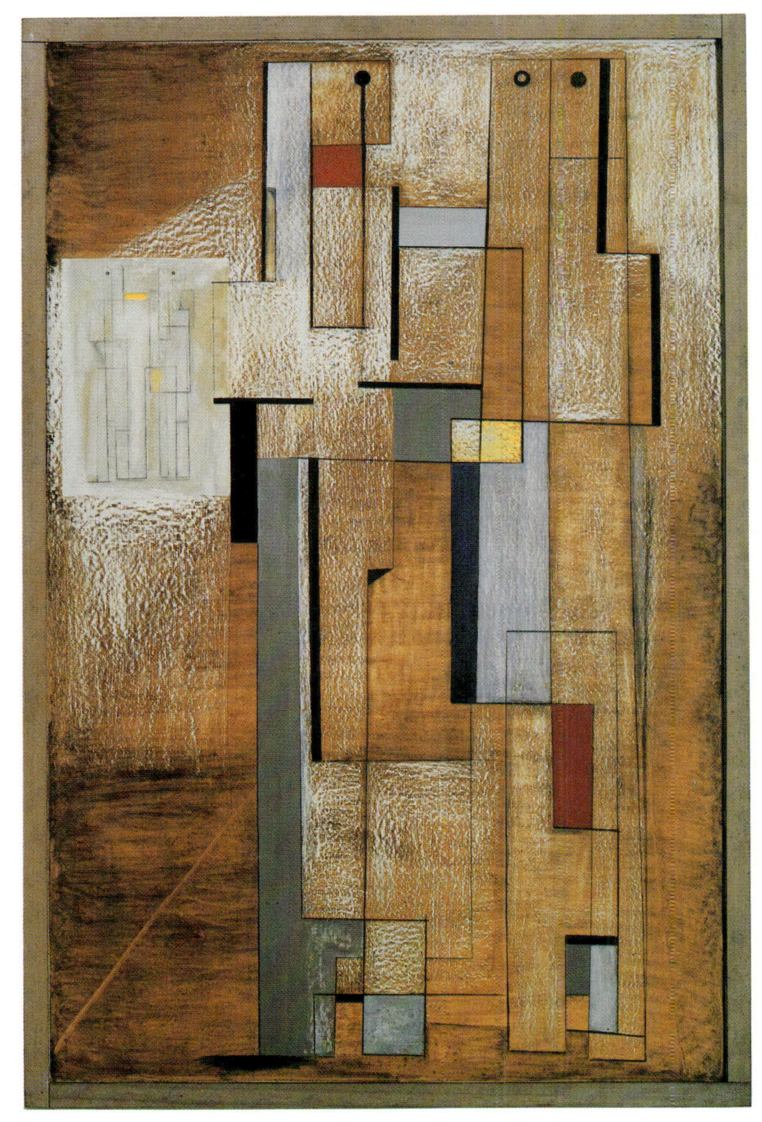

□ **Two Figures (Heroes)** 1954

left
□ **Makutu** 1969
right
□ **Oval with Two Forms** 1971

below left
Rock Face 1973
below right
Touchstone 1969

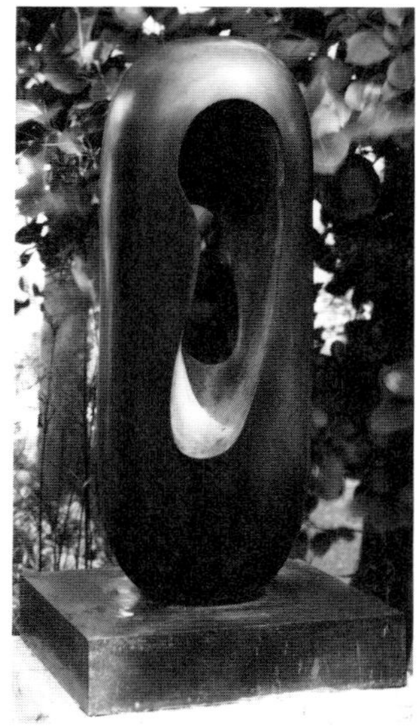

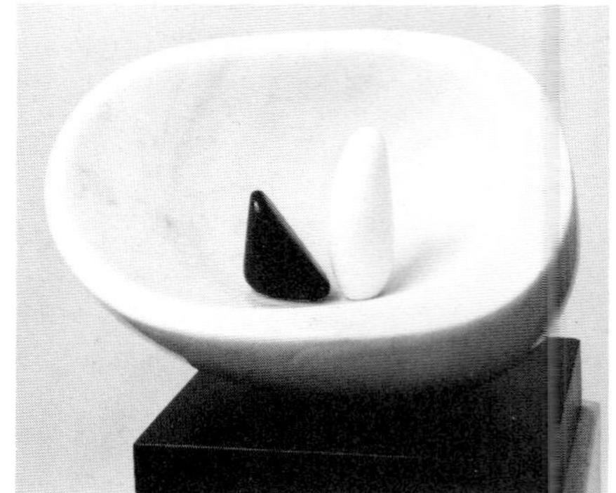

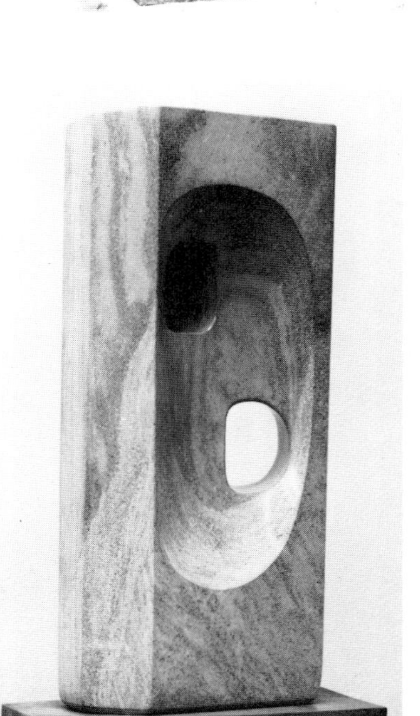

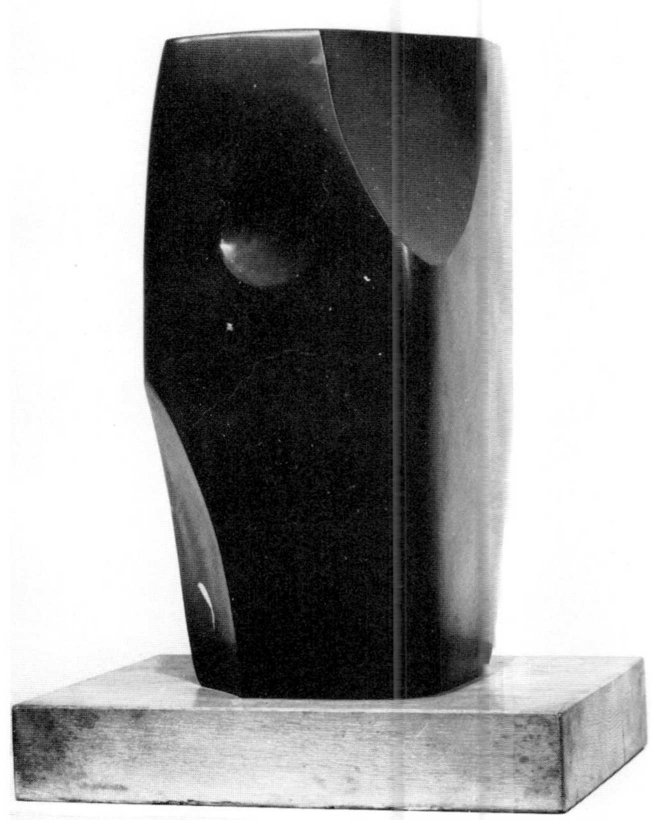

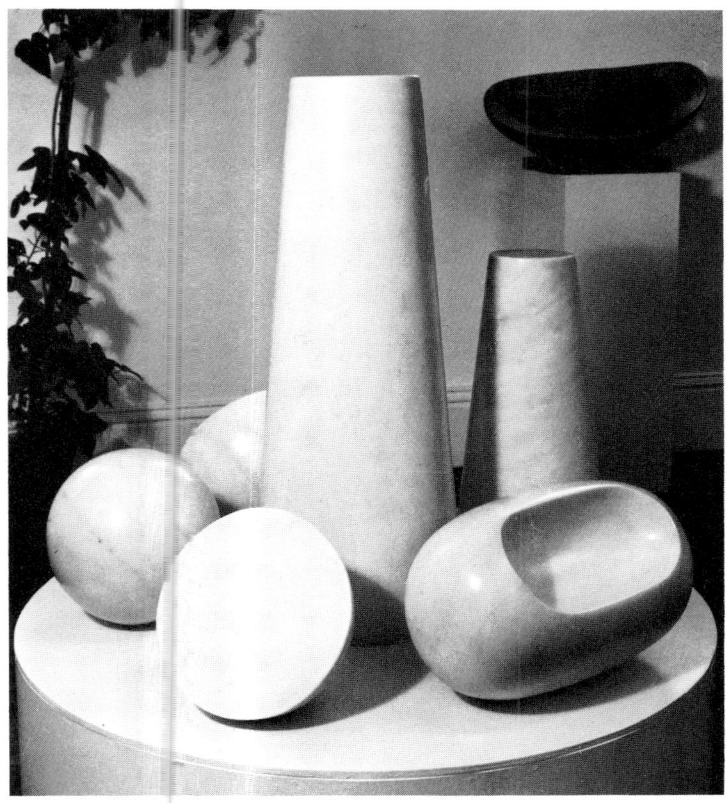

□ **Fallen Images** 1974–5

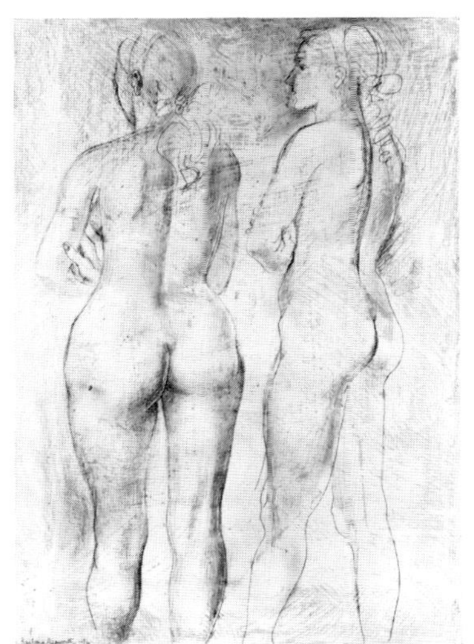

Two Figures with Folded Arms 1947

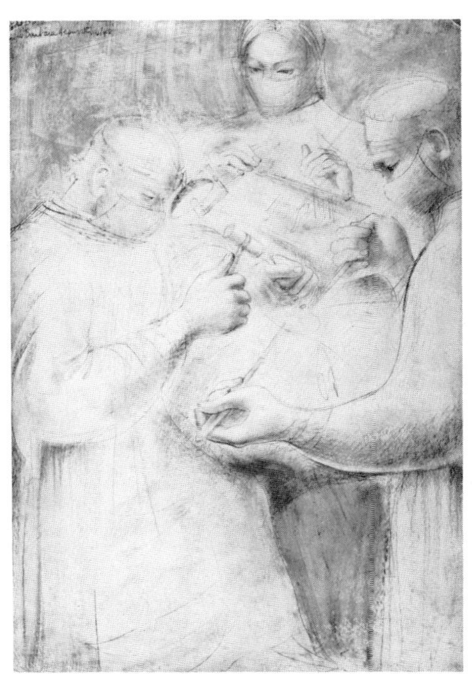

Fenestration of the Ear (The Hammer) 1948

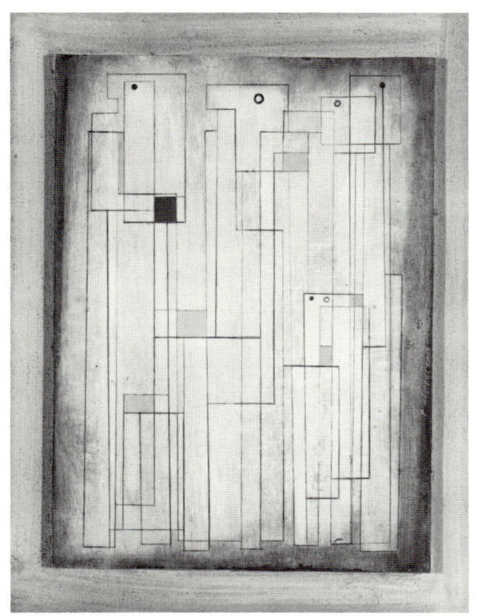

left
Family Group, Earth Red and Yellow 1953

right
Two Forms (White and Yellow) 1955

below left
Perigord 1958

below right
Forms (West Penwith) 1958

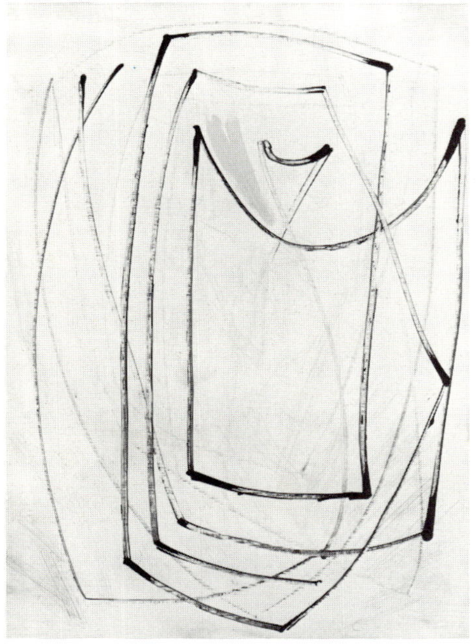

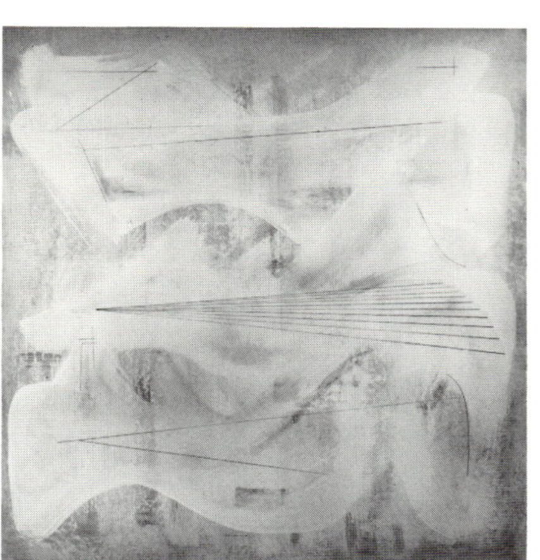

Carving studio, St Ives

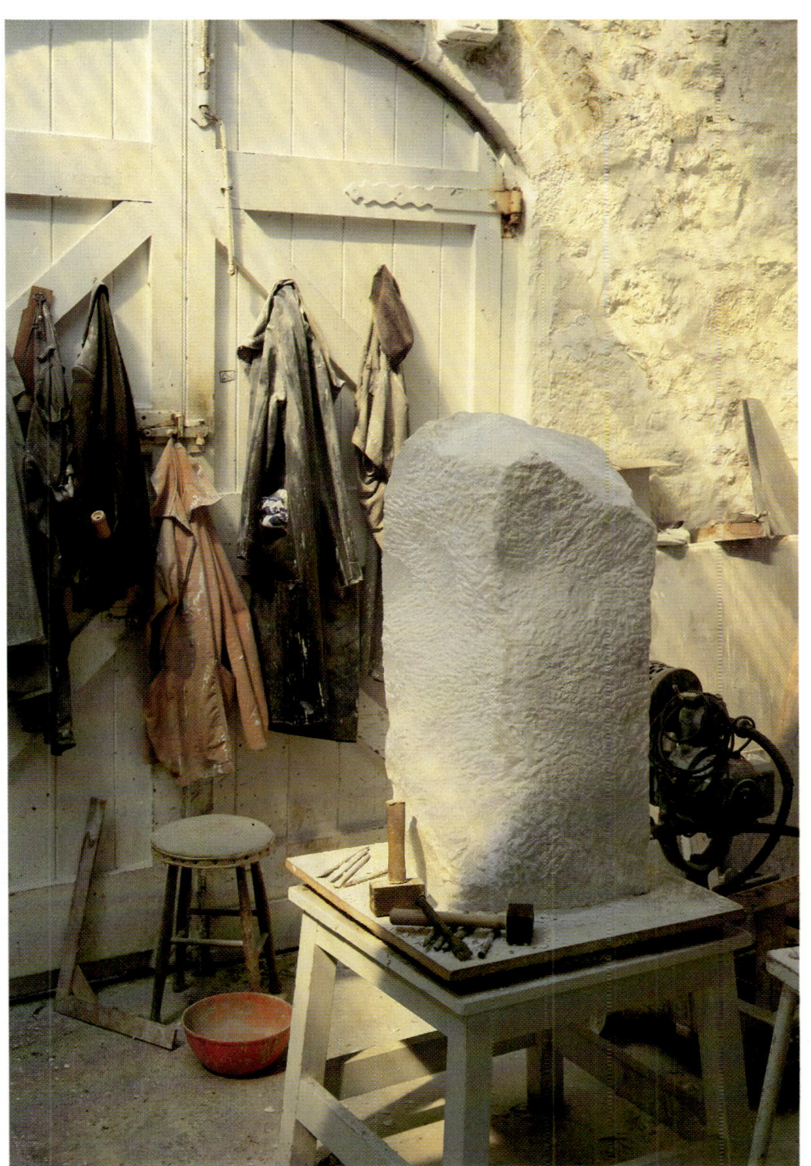

Complete list of the Tate Gallery Collection, 1982

Works at St Ives are marked □, and were presented by the Executors of the Artist's Estate 1980.
References are to Tate Gallery catalogue numbers, and Barbara Hepworth's own catalogue of her sculptures.
Measurements are given in inches followed by centimetres in brackets.

SCULPTURE

1928

□ **Torso**

Hoptonwood stone
14¼ × 6¾ × 4 (36 × 17 × 10)
T.3128 (BH 12)

1929

□ **Infant**

Burmese wood
17¼ × 10¾ × 10
(43.5 × 27.3 × 25.4)
T.3129 (BH 24)

1929–30

Figure of a Woman

Corsehill stone
21¾ × 13 × 13¾
(55.5 × 33 × 35)
Presented by the artist 1967
T.952 (BH 27)

1932–3

□ **Seated Figure**

Lignum vitae
14 × 10½ × 8
(35.6 × 26.7 × 21.6)
T.3130 (BH 46)

1934

□ **Three Forms**

Grey alabaster
10⅜ × 18⅛ × 8⅝
(26.3 × 47.3 × 21.7)
T.3131 (BH 66)

1935

Three Forms

Serravezza marble
7¾ × 21 × 13½ (20 × 53.5 × 34)
Presented by Mr and Mrs J.R. Marcus Brumwell 1964
T.696 (BH 72)

□ **Discs in Echelon**

Bronze (cast 1959)
13½ × 19⅞ × 10¾
(34.3 × 50.5 × 27.3)
T.3132 (BH 73iv)

1936

Ball, Plane and Hole

Teak wood
8 × 24 × 12
(20.4 × 61.1 × 30.5)
Purchased 1982
T.3399

1937–8

Single Form (Eikon)

Bronze (cast 1963)
58¼ × 11 × 12½ (147 × 28 × 32)
Presented by the artist 1964
T.697 (BH 104)

1938

Forms in Echelon

Tulip wood
41¾ × 23½ × 27¾
(106 × 59.5 × 70.5)
Presented by the artist 1964
T.698 (BH 107)

1940

□ **Sculpture with Colour, Deep Blue and Red**

Plaster and string
4⅛ × 5⅞ × 4⅛ (10.5 × 15 × 10.6)
T.3133 (BH 117)

1943

Oval Sculpture (No.2)

Plaster (made in 1958)
11¼ × 16¼ × 10
(28.5 × 41.5 × 25.5)
Presented by the artist 1967
T.953 (BH 121)

1943–4

□ **The Artist's Hand**

Bronze (cast 1967)
2⅜ × 7½ × 4 (6 × 19 × 10)
T.3154 (BH 4[illegible]4)

1944

Landscape Sculpture

Bronze (cast 1961)
12½ × 25¾ × [illegible]1
(32 × 65.5 × 2[illegible])
Presented by the artist 1967
T.954 (BH 127)

1946

Pelagos

Wood and strings
14½ × 15¼ × [illegible]3 (37 × 39 × 33)
Presented by the artist 1964
T.699 (BH 13[illegible])

Tides I

Holly wood
13¼ × 24¾ × 1[illegible]
(33.5 × 63 × 2[illegible])
Presented by Ben Nicholson, O.M. 1975
T.2008 (BH 1[illegible]9)

1949

Bicentric Form

Blue limestone
$62\frac{1}{2} \times 19 \times 12\frac{1}{2}$ (159 × 48 × 31)
Purchased 1950
5932 (BH 160)

1951

Group I (Concourse), February 4 1951

Serravezza marble
$9\frac{3}{4} \times 19\frac{3}{4} \times 11\frac{3}{4}$
(24.7 × 50.5 × 29.5)
Bequeathed by Miss E.M. Hodgkins 1977
T.2226 (BH 171)

1951–2 and 1957

□ **Poised Form**

Blue marble
$46 \times 17\frac{7}{8} \times 15$
(117 × 45.5 × 38)
T.3134 (BH 172)

1954–5

Corinthos

Nigerian scented guarea wood
41 × 42 × 40
(104 × 107 × 102)
Purchased 1962
T.531 (BH 198)

1955–6

□ **Coré**

Bronze (cast 1960)
$29\frac{1}{4} \times 15\frac{3}{4} \times 11\frac{3}{4}$ (74 × 40 × 30)
T.3135 (BH 208 (marble))

1956

Orpheus (Maquette 2, version II)

Brass and string
$45\frac{1}{4} \times 17 \times 16\frac{1}{4}$
(115 × 43 × 41.5)
Presented by the artist 1967
T.955 (BH 222)

□ **Forms in Movement (Pavan)**

Bronze (cast 1967)
$27\frac{1}{2} \times 42\frac{1}{2} \times 23$
(70 × 108 × 58.5)
T.3136 (BH 453)

□ **Stringed Figure (Curlew), version II**

Brass and string
$20\frac{1}{4} \times 30\frac{1}{4} \times 17$
(51.3 × 77 × 43)
T.3137 (BH 225ii)

Curved Form (Travalgan)

Bronze
$35\frac{1}{2} \times 23\frac{1}{2} \times 26\frac{1}{2}$ (90 × 60 × 67)
Purchased 1960
T.353 (BH 213)

1958

□ **Torso II (Torcello)**

Bronze
$34\frac{3}{4} \times 11\frac{3}{4} \times 11$ (88 × 30 × 28)
T.3138 (BH 234)

□ **Garden Sculpture (Model for Meridian)**

Bronze
$63 \times 31\frac{1}{2} \times 11\frac{3}{4}$ (160 × 80 × 30)
T.3139 (BH 246)

Figure (Nanjizal)

Yew wood
$102\frac{1}{2} \times 35\frac{3}{4} \times 23\frac{3}{4}$
(260 × 91 × 60)
Purchased 1960
T.352 (BH 236)

Cantate Domino

Bronze
$82\frac{1}{4} \times 20\frac{3}{4} \times 19\frac{3}{4}$
(209 × 53 × 50)
Presented by the artist 1967
T.956 (BH 244)

Sea Form (Porthmeor)

Bronze
$30\frac{1}{4} \times 44\frac{3}{4} \times 10$
(67 × 114 × 25.5)
Presented by the artist 1967
T.957 (BH 249)

1959–60

Figure (Nyanga)

Elm wood
$35\frac{3}{4} \times 22\frac{1}{2} \times 11\frac{3}{4}$
(91 × 57 × 29.8)
Presented by the artist 1969
T.1112 (BH 273)

1960

□ **Figure for Landscape**

Bronze
$102\frac{1}{2} \times 49\frac{1}{4} \times 26\frac{1}{2}$
(260 × 125 × 67.5)
T.3140 (BH 287)

□ **Pierced Form (Epidauros)**

Nigerian scented guarea wood
$29 \times 26\frac{1}{2} \times 13\frac{3}{4}$
(73.6 × 67.6 × 34.7)
T.3141 (BH 290)

Image II

White marble
$29\frac{1}{2} \times 30\frac{1}{2} \times 19$
(75 × 77.5 × 48)
Presented by the artist 1967
T.958 (BH 277)

1961

□ **Maquette, Three Forms in Echelon**

Brass and string on a wooden board
$26\frac{3}{4} \times 20\frac{1}{2} \times 8\frac{1}{2}$
(68 × 52.2 × 21.7)
T.3142 (BH 306)

Maquette, Three Forms in Echelon

Bronze (cast 1965)
$26\frac{3}{4} \times 20 \times 3\frac{3}{4}$ (68 × 51 × 9.5)
Presented by the artist 1967
T.959 (BH, under 306)

□ **Single Form (September)**

Walnut wood
$32\frac{1}{2} \times 20 \times 2\frac{1}{4}$
(82.7 × 50.5 × 5.7)
T.3141 (BH 312)

1962

□ **Square Forms**

Bronze
$13\frac{1}{4} \times 7\frac{1}{2} \times 3\frac{1}{2}$ (33.5 × 19 × 9)
T.3144 (BH 313)

1962–3

□ **Bronze Form (Patmos)**

Bronze
$25\frac{3}{4} \times 37\frac{1}{2} \times 9\frac{1}{2}$
(65.5 × 95 × 24)
T.3145 (BH 321)

1963

□ **Sphere with Inner Form**

Bronze
$38\frac{1}{2} \times 35\frac{1}{2} \times 31\frac{1}{2}$
(97.5 × 90 × 80)
T.3146 (BH 333)

1963 (cont.)

□ **Squares with Two Circles**

Bronze
$125\frac{1}{2} \times 63 \times 30\frac{1}{4}$
(330 × 160 × 77)
Purchased 1964
T.702 (BH 347)

1963–4

Pierced Form

Pentelicon marble
$49\frac{3}{4} \times 38\frac{1}{4} \times 9$ (126 × 97 × 23)
Presented by the artist 1964
T.704 (BH 350)

1964

Two Figures (Menhirs)

Slate
$32\frac{1}{2} \times 25 \times 13$
(82.5 × 63.5 × 33)
Purchased 1964
T.703 (BH 361)

1965

Hollow Form with White (Elegy III)

Elm wood
$53 \times 23 \times 18\frac{1}{4}$
(134.5 × 59 × 46.5)
Presented by the artist 1967
T.960 (BH 384)

1968

□ **Six Forms (2 × 3)**

Bronze
$22\frac{1}{2} \times 34\frac{1}{2} \times 13\frac{1}{4}$
(57.2 × 87.5 × 33.7)
T.3147 (BH 467)

□ **Hollow Form with Inner Form**

Bronze
$48\frac{1}{2} \times 26 \times 26$ (123 × 66 × 66)
T.3148 (BH 469)

□ **Vertical Form (St Ives)**

Bronze (cast 1969)
$18\frac{1}{2} \times 10 \times 4$ (47 × 25.7 × 10)
T.3150 (BH 495)

1969

□ **Two Forms (Divided Circle)**

Bronze
$93\frac{1}{2} \times 92 \times 21\frac{1}{4}$
(237 × 234 × 54.3)
T.3149 (BH 477)

□ **Makutu**

Bronze (cast 1970)
$26\frac{1}{2} \times 9\frac{3}{4} \times 9\frac{3}{4}$
(67.5 × 24.5 × 24.3)
T.3151 (BH 505)

Touchstone

Irish black marble
$24\frac{3}{4} \times 12 \times 14\frac{3}{4}$
(63 × 30.5 × 37)
Bequeathed by the artist 1975
T.2016 (BH 496)

1971

□ **Oval with Two Forms**

White marble and slate
$13\frac{1}{4} \times 15\frac{1}{2} \times 13$
(33.5 × 39 × 33)
T.3152 (BH 525)

1973

Rock Face

Ancaster stone
$40\frac{1}{2} \times 18\frac{1}{2} \times 8\frac{1}{2}$
(102.9 × 47 × 21.6)
Bequeathed by the artist 1975
T.2017 (BH 560)

1974–5

□ **Fallen Images**

White marble
$48 \times 51\frac{1}{4} \times 51\frac{1}{4}$
(122 × 130 × 130)
T.3153 (BH 574)

OIL PAINTINGS AND DRAWINGS

1947

Two Figures with Folded Arms

Oil and pencil on wood
14 × 10 (35.5 × 25.5)
Purchased 1959
T.269

1948

Fenestration of the Ear (The Hammer)

Oil and pencil on board
$15\frac{1}{8} \times 10\frac{5}{8}$ (38.4 × 27)
Purchased 1976
T.2098

1953

Family Group, Earth Red and Yellow

Oil and pencil on hardboard
$11\frac{3}{4} \times 8\frac{3}{4}$ (30 × 22.3)
Bequeathed by Miss E.M. Hodgkins 1977
T.2228

1954

□ **Two Figures (Heroes)**

Oil on board
72 × 48 (183 × 122)
T.3155

1955

Two Forms (White and Yellow)

Oil and pencil on hardboard
$16\frac{3}{4} \times 6$ (42.5 × 15.2)
Bequeathed by Miss E.M. Hodgkins 1977
T.2227

1958

Perigord

Oil and ink on hardboard
$19 \times 14\frac{1}{4}$ (48 × 36)
Presented by the artist 1964
T.701

Forms (West Penwith)

Oil and pencil on hardboard
$25\frac{1}{4} \times 25$ (64 × 63.5)
Presented by the artist 1964
T.700